T0295745

Making History

ABOUT THE SERIES

The American Association for State and Local History Book Series addresses issues critical to the field of state and local history through interpretive, intellectual, scholarly, and educational texts. To submit a proposal or manuscript to the series, please request proposal guidelines from AASLH headquarters: AASLH Editorial Board, 2021 21st Ave. South, Suite 320, Nashville, Tennessee 37212. Telephone: (615) 320-3203. Website: www.aaslh.org.

ABOUT THE ORGANIZATION

The American Association for State and Local History (AASLH) is a national history membership association headquartered in Nashville, Tennessee, that provides leadership and support for its members who preserve and interpret state and local history in order to make the past more meaningful to all people. AASLH members are leaders in preserving, researching, and interpreting traces of the American past to connect the people, thoughts, and events of yesterday with the creative memories and abiding concerns of people, communities, and our nation today. In addition to sponsorship of this book series, AASLH publishes *History News* magazine, a newsletter, technical leaflets and reports, and other materials; confers prizes and awards in recognition of outstanding achievement in the field; supports a broad education program and other activities designed to help members work more effectively; and advocates on behalf of the discipline of history. To join AASLH, go to www.aaslh.org or contact Membership Services, AASLH, 2021 21st Ave. South, Suite 320, Nashville, TN 37212.

Making History
Makerspaces for Museums and Historic Sites

Tim Betz

ROWMAN & LITTLEFIELD
Lanham • Boulder • New York • London

Published by Rowman & Littlefield
An imprint of The Rowman & Littlefield Publishing Group, Inc.
4501 Forbes Boulevard, Suite 200, Lanham, Maryland 20706
www.rowman.com

86-90 Paul Street, London EC2A 4NE

British Library Cataloguing in Publication Information Available

Library of Congress Cataloging-in-Publication Data

Names: Betz, Tim, 1989- author. | American Association for State and Local History.
Title: Making history : makerspaces for museums and historic sites / Tim Betz.
Other titles: Makerspaces for museums and historic sites
Description: Lanham : Rowman & Littlefield, [2023] | Series: American Association for State and Local History book series | Includes bibliographical references and index. | Summary: "While first person interpretation and historic crafts have long been part of the museum world, current movements in the maker movement in libraries and schools have occurred mostly outside of the museum world. Instead, "Makerspace in Museums: Hands-On History in Museums and Historic Sites" shows the importance of the Maker Movement for museums and historic sites, and presents a roadmap to building, planning, researching, and using a makerspace alongside more traditional museum programming. It calls for a revitalization of living history, which can be done through makerspaces and the maker movement."— Provided by publisher.
Identifiers: LCCN 2022053055 (print) | LCCN 2022053056 (ebook) | ISBN 9781538169018 (cloth ; alk. paper) | ISBN 9781538169025 (paper ; alk. paper) | ISBN 9781538169032 (electronic)
Subjects: LCSH: Makerspaces in museums. | Museums—Educational aspects. | Historic sites—Educational aspects. | Maker movement. | History—Study and teaching.
Classification: LCC AM124.37 .B48 2023 (print) | LCC AM124.37 (ebook) | DDC 069/.1—dc23/eng/20230306
LC record available at https://lccn.loc.gov/2022053055
LC ebook record available at https://lccn.loc.gov/2022053056

For my grandfather who taught me to make,

And for Chelsea who encouraged me to make this.

Contents

Acknowledgments

No book happens alone, and this is not an exception. I have many people to thank who helped make this project possible.

The museum field is small, but the museum field is generous. I have had the great fortune of talking with people who, kindly and graciously, gave of their time to help make this project the best it could be. Among them are Shaun Pekar, Mark Hutter, Kristie Truluck, Sarah Woodyard, Sarah Kirk, Rebecca Martin, Asher Lurie, Ryan Paxton, and Andrew Sargent. I am also indebted to museum professionals and historians from throughout North America who filled out my survey form asking strange questions about making, museums, and history. Of these, I am particularly thankful to those who took part in my "Makerspaces in History Museums" all-day workshop at the AASLH conference in Buffalo, New York, in September 2022 as I was finishing the final edits for this book. Their insight, questions, enthusiasm, and perspectives allowed me to think about this project in new ways and to see it through new eyes. I am also thankful for the aid of Kris Jackson at the VR studio at Goggleworks Center for the Arts. What great company I keep in this strange, important, and sometimes frustrating field!

Thanks to the team at Rowman & Littlefield, particularly Charles Harmon and Erinn Slanina. Also, thanks to AASLH, especially Aja Bain, who has been a cheerful advocate of this project from the beginning. Thanks for seeing this as a worthwhile project and for helping to make it better at every step.

I am thankful for my friends in academia, a happy second home for me. I am thankful for the support of the Art History "A Team" at Kutztown University: it is a pleasure to be a part of you. I am grateful for my students, who inspire me every day. I am also thankful for the support, mentorship, and constant advocacy of Bárbara Zepeda, my dissertation advisor at Lehigh University who encouraged me to take up a book project while I was also writing my dissertation on a completely unrelated topic. *Gracias, Bárbara.*

I am thankful for my team at the Morgan Log House, especially to Kristi Chase, who was with me with the Morgan Log House Makerspace from the beginning and joined me for many fascinating journeys into the historic processes of the past.

Particular thanks to Tim Compton, who helped me question this project and helped make it better over many glasses of craft beer. Told you I'd make something eventually!

The most thanks I have is for my wife, Chelsea, without whom I would not be who I am today. Thanks for pushing me further, for pushing this project further, and for helping me come out of a pandemic better than when I entered it.

Thanks, also, to Annie and Henry, who sat with me to write every chapter, and to Alfred, who joined me at the very end.

Introduction

This is a book about making history, but not quite what that usually means. It is a manifesto, a theoretical framework, and a call to action. History should not just be observed; history should be experienced. A visitor to a historic site should not just look at the past; they should get their hands dirty in it. This book, *Making History: Makerspaces for Museums and Historic Sites*, asserts that the ideas of the makerspace, usually confined to STEM learning and education, should be applied to historic sites as well; that visitors of any age at historic sites should be given a space to learn about the past by using the historic techniques of the past.

To install a historic makerspace at a historic site is an acceptance of the ethos of making. It is a statement that your historic site believes that people should be able to experience the past for themselves rather than simply be told about it.

This is more than just butter churning or using a spinning wheel (although those might be a site's or its visitors' entrance into making). At a historic makerspace, the past comes alive. Makers learn and research historic trades and crafts and apply them to the modern world. People encounter the museum as a place that is full of life, dynamic and for everyone. Researchers can embrace the physicality of the world of the past and use it as a tool for understanding the lives of people who had come before.

ABOUT ME

I might not have realized it, but I've been a maker my whole life. My grandfather was a sign painter, an artist, and a tinkerer, and taught me how to make things from a very young age. I received an education in studio art from Kutztown University of Pennsylvania, a master's in art history from Penn State, a master's in history from Lehigh University, and, as of this writing, am working on my PhD at Lehigh as well. I teach art history at Kutztown University and I am a museum professional, having served in many capacities in small museums. I am an artist, a beekeeper, and like to garden and brew beer.

But why all this about me? For much of my life of working as an academic and scholar of history, I have worked to separate the two: to separate Tim the artist and maker from Tim the historian, museum professional, and scholar. To see these as two separate pursuits that are both rewarding but with not much overlap between them. This book, in part, is an answer to this problem; it was born of a realization I had that these two things don't need to be separate. Tim the maker could also be Tim the historian, Tim the scholar. The museum did not need to be a static place where people encounter objects on the wall and learn about them. The museum could be a place where people learn about how to make things by using the tools and techniques of the past. The classroom could be a place where people could learn about the past by making and doing. The world of the past existed in tangible reality: people got their hands dirty in the stuff of the past. We should get our hands dirty when we learn about the past, too.

My first historic makerspace, the Morgan Log House Makerspace, at the Morgan Log House in Lansdale, Pennsylvania, began as a necessity during the shutdowns of the COVID-19 pandemic in the beginning of the long year of 2020. Without having tours on-site, we needed to have a way to engage our community and visitors with the past. The answer was to get their hands dirty (something that everyone was avoiding that year). Craft kits and outdoor maker programs evolved into a regular schedule of making programs and maker-centric offerings. It became clear that people of all sorts, from the young to the old, wanted to make, and they wanted a space to make that was safe, friendly, and supportive.

The historic makerspace is just that space. It is a space for people of any age or background to gather and learn together. A place to find a friendly and supportive space to try, succeed, and fail. A place to interact with the past and to bring it into the present, to question traditional narratives and challenge the structures of history which have formed an unjust society. One could say that "it's just making a craft," but it's more than that; it's making a space for encountering the past and ourselves. In a modern world full of polarization and deep-seated anger and animosity, providing a space that is safe to learn and grow as a community is of the highest importance. A museum can do that. A historic site can do that. A historic makerspace can do that.

A NOTE ON HISTORIC MAKING

This book calls for the use of historic making as a tool for making historic sites more dynamic and for engaging the public in new ways. While the concept of historic making will be discussed further, I believe it is helpful to describe what historic making is.

Historic making is understanding that the past is a dynamic place and that it can be interacted with, taught about, and better understood by learning a historic trade or craft. A historic maker gets their hands dirty and learns a skill. Sometimes they learn it to the high degree of a craftsman. Sometimes they learn it well enough to teach it as a workshop. Sometimes they learn it as a research tool. In the end, historic making is a tactile exploration of the ways in which people in the past lived and encountered the world around them. It provides a place where people can find empathy with people who lived in the past and who live with us in the present, united across time and space by the human desire to make something.

Historical making builds off the successes of the Maker Movement and applies them to understanding the processes of making in the past, using the very modern and digital idea of the Maker Movement and the makerspace to understanding and encountering history. Historical making works to understand and acknowledge the problems inherent in the Maker Movement (such as sexism, racism, classism, and an over-focusing on capitalist outcomes), as well as the challenges of the museum field and the world of history, and works toward solving them through human interaction. Historic making, finally, acknowledges that the historic trades of the past are precious living artifacts that should be preserved, used, and interacted with, to learn about the past, the present, and the future.

Historic making is a way to look at the museum and the past as alive, dynamic, and engaging.

HOW TO USE THIS BOOK

This book is a guide for understanding makerspaces and the Maker Movement and using that knowledge to craft a historic makerspace at a historic site. Parts of it are theoretical and ask philosophical questions about what a museum is and what it means to make. Others are more practical and provide a framework to help build a historic makerspace at a museum or historic site. Both the theoretical/philosophical and the practical are important. It is important to understand the whys as much as it is to understand the hows.

This book can be used to help steer a historic site toward the creation of a historic makerspace that is used on-site regularly. It can be used as a guide to create a temporary makerspace. It can be used as a guide for the creating of a program that a historic site tries just once. It can be all, it can be a little, or it can be nothing at all. Jumping into this book is not necessarily jumping into creating a makerspace at your site (though I hope it will certainly get you to think about it). Rather, it is a call to action for your historic site: Why not let people get their hands dirty?

This book is broken up into three sections.

The first three chapters are concerned with the theoretical and the history of the makerspace. They analyze the Maker Movement, with all its potential and all its flaws (chapter 1), they make a case for bringing the Maker Movement into the world of museums and historic sites (chapter 2), and they present a pedagogy for making at a museum or historic site (chapter 3).

The next two chapters are practical and talk about the process of making a historic makerspace (chapter 4) and programming in the makerspace (chapter

5). They help provide a background into the process of bringing a makerspace into physical reality and what to do with it once you have one.

The final two chapters are an assertion that making is a form of research, for museum professionals, for historians, and for the public. Chapter 6 discusses the processes of learning a historic trade or craft and some of the problems that can arise throughout the process. Chapter 7 talks about historic making as the preservation of cultural heritage and argues that learning by making is an important tool for researching the complexities of the past; it can also help bring voices to life who have been previously silenced by the text of history.

This book ends with several appendices, which provide helpful resources for making a makerspace, including sample surveys, questionnaires, assessment tools, and resources for making, as well as some easy recipes and projects to get you started.

Let's make some history!

1

Makerspaces and the Maker Movement

Before we bring the Maker Movement into the world of history museums and historic making, we will first explore the idea of the Maker Movement and the tradition of the makerspace, as well as some critiques of the Maker Movement. This chapter will explore how museums and historic sites' engagement with the Maker Movement can be mutually beneficial for both the sites and the movement. History and historic sites are particularly well suited to answering the critiques and problems of the Maker Movement.

THE MAKER MOVEMENT

The origins of the Maker Movement began around 2005, with the creation of *Make* magazine by Dale Dougherty, Sherry Huss, Dan Woods, and Tim O'Reilly.[1] The group modeled their magazine on the classic magazine *Popular Mechanics*, which introduced the idea of making and tinkering to a home audience at the beginning of the twentieth century. Soon, the Maker Movement became social with events such as the Maker Faire, the first of which was held in April 2006 in San Mateo, California, which developed as a gathering of makers and a celebration of the idea of making. The Maker Faire was "an eclectic mix of people, projects, and things, the twenty-first century version of the state fair was born."[2] From the beginning, then, the Maker Movement was inherently social.

It was also tied to the idea of making something tangible. The Maker Movement's makers create physical things rather than just pixels on a screen, atoms rather than bits, and use the tools of software to revolutionize the ways in which tangible objects are made.[3]

Soon after it formed, Makerspaces began appearing in public libraries, science museums, and schools. The Maker Movement, growing out of the introduction of new technologies and the do-it-yourself (DIY) era, had become fully intertwined with the teaching philosophy of STEM (Science, Technology, Engineering, and Math), which became all-encompassing in American education in the early 2000s. The Maker Movement gained traction as a way to interact with STEM fields that emphasized fun, collaboration, and communal growth. In part, this was to answer an essential problem of American manufacturing, which was that more traditional educational programs were not feeding enough students into careers in manufacturing. STEM education placed emphasis on the sciences, which, in turn, placed emphasis on American manufacturing. As Barack Obama told participants at the first White House Maker Faire in 2014, "Today's DIY is tomorrow's 'Made in America'. . . . Your projects are examples of a revolution that's taking place in American manufacturing—a revolution that can help us create new jobs and industries for decades to come."[4] Thanks to the Obama White House's focus on the Maker Movement through initiatives such as the White House Maker Faire, the Maker Movement could lead to a renaissance of American manufacturing. As Chris Anderson has noted in *Makers: The New Industrial Revolution*, the Maker Movement represents a rapid departure from the previous modes of established manufacturing, and has democratized the idea of the factory and the idea of making. He notes that "the beauty of the Web is that it democratized the tools both of invention and of production. Anyone with an idea for a service can turn it into a product with some software code (these days it hardly even requires much programming skill, and what you need you can learn online)—no patent required. Then with a keystroke, you can 'ship it' to a global market of billions of people."[5] The main defining ethos of the Maker Movement for people like Anderson is the idea that technology will bring about democratization of what it means to be a producer, a maker. The Maker Movement focuses on the egalitarian and open-source nature of the digital world. For proponents of the movement, the readily available nature of technology makes that technology more accessible to everyone. Therefore, the Maker Movement, in its ideal, is for everyone, in part because technology is readily available to everyone. As has been discussed above, though, the ideals of the Maker Movement—of egalitarian access, of exploration, of education—quickly could become intertwined with money and the manufacturing sector.

The Maker Movement is tied to technology, and through the use of technology can create a better world. Part of what makes that world better is the ready access of materials, technology, and information in places like makerspaces. A digital world (which is becoming increasingly more digital with movements toward the Metaverse) provides a place for people to make, grow, and learn together. On its face, this is exciting and new.

As will be explored later in this chapter, though, the Maker Movement does not hold up to its ideals of egalitarian technology for all.

A GENEALOGY OF THE MAKER MOVEMENT

The Maker Movement has hands-on precursors that played a role in forming the movement as we know it today. Outside of understanding what the Maker Movement is today, these other examples show where the Maker Movement originated. This can help us to understand the contours and realities of what it means to be a maker. Making is far more than technology. It's an ethos. There are important precursors to the digital focus of the current makerspace. These precursors to the movement are frequently ignored. Many Maker Movement histories begin with Dale Dougherty's *Make* magazine in 2005, as mine did. In reality, the origins go much further.

Some of the genetics of the Maker Movement can trace themselves to other places. One element could be the Arts and Crafts Movement of the late nineteenth century. The Arts and Crafts Movement originated in England around a circle of artists and craftsmen that included William Morris (1834–1896) and John Ruskin (1819–1900). The Arts and Crafts Movement quickly gained traction in other parts of the world, especially the United States with artists like Arthur Wesley Dow (1857–1922) and Pedro Joseph de Lemos (1882–1954). The Arts and Crafts Movement was a purposeful shift away from manufacturing and mass production and focused on the creation of materials that were made by hand; it was a celebration of the handmade and of the skills of the artisan, which was wrapped into socialist ideologies that were on the rise at the industrial turn of the century. Those who were part of the Arts and Crafts Movement worked in a variety of traditional mediums and trades, finding inspiration in the processes of making of the past, a past which was before the factory and the steam engine.[6] The Arts and Crafts Movement was a celebration of the maker and the skills of the maker. While most certainly it was connected to the political and social ideologies of its members, it was very assuredly a movement that was centered on the idea of making. The Arts and Crafts Movement is not something that is typically considered to be part of the genetic makeup of the modern Maker Movement; in many ways, it was directly opposed to some of the Maker Movement's more capitalistic urges. However, at its heart, it was about changing the world through making, and through a community of making.

The Maker Movement takes the idea of tinkering and making in a solitary workshop and centers it around a community, an idea that was given voice in the Men's Shed Movement that originated in Australia in the 1980s. The goal of the Men's Shed Movement is to provide a space for craft and for social interaction. While it was originally meant to be a place for older (usually retired) men to engage with each other, many men's sheds allow admission to anyone, regardless of age or gender.[7] The Men's Shed Movement seems to have formed among a community of retired miners in New South Wales, Australia, in 1978, with a concept of providing a place similar to a backyard shed, where men could tinker together. This was made concrete in 2002, with the formation of Mensheds Australia, a non-profit organization which oversees men's sheds. This was shortly followed by the Australian Men's Shed Association in 2007.[8] At its heart, the Men's Shed Movement is a place for the mental and physical well-being of older men, who often find themselves without a space for social interaction. Most certainly, the Men's Shed Movement has provided a space for "shedders" (the name for users of the shed) to gather and work together, which is encapsulated by the organization's current motto, "Shoulder to shoulder," which is shortened from "Men don't talk face to face, they talk shoulder to shoulder."[9] The Men's Shed Movement is an interesting point of consideration for the genealogy of the Maker Movement. In part, this is because it hones in on some of the good things the Maker Movement is about, such as communal making and providing a space for the community to come together. It also shows some of the problems of the Maker Movement (which will be discussed later in this chapter), which include underserving women and people of color. While the Men's Shed Movement has taken important steps to include everyone, barriers of entry for women and people of color is an unfortunate element of the Maker Movement.

Most certainly, the Men's Shed Movement owes some of its own genetics to the ever-growing DIY movement of the twentieth century. In the modern world, the idea of do-it-yourself is everywhere; there are even television networks about it. What we think of as the DIY Movement was part of the patterns of self-sufficiency which began in the postwar period, with increased numbers of people taking part in personal projects, including home renovation and construction. This originated from pre-war magazines such as *Popular Mechanics* (1902), which eventually formed the basis for *Make* magazine, one of the originating factors of the modern Maker Movement, and the publication of books such as C. T. Shaefer's *The Handyman's Handbook* in 1931, the first how-to book for home maintenance and the more readily accessible nature of power tools. In part, the Do-It-Yourself Movement was tied to mid-century movements of self-sufficiency as well as a fear that, in an increasingly mechanized world, traditional skills and self-sufficiency were at risk. These fears were voiced by Alan Watts, who, in 1967, noted, "Our educational system, in its entirety, does nothing to give us any kind of material competence. In other words, we don't learn how to cook, how to make clothes, how to build houses, how to make love, or to do any of the absolutely fundamental things of life. The whole education that we get for our children in school is entirely in terms of abstractions. It trains you to be an insurance salesman or a bureaucrat, or some kind of cerebral character."[10] The Do-It-Yourself Movement was connected to both twentieth-century hope and twentieth-century fear.

These three examples—the Arts and Crafts Movement, the Men's Shed Movement, and the Do-It-Yourself Movement—are but a selection of the precursors to what we would identify as the Maker Movement. Likewise, they tell us a lot about what the Maker Movement is about outside of technology and innovation. First, it's about the formation of a community. In that community, like-minded makers work toward building a common goal. Second, it's about the process of making as well as the finished result. The road to making is as important as the finished destination. Finally, it is about the preservation, education, and passing on of craft. Often centered around anxieties connected to loss, these earlier Maker Movements are connected to learning and passing on knowledge, and using that knowledge to reach a common goal. This longer genealogy of what we can call the Maker Movement also shows that the idea of a community of makers working together is not new. This framework has existed for centuries, and has been used by craftsman, makers, and tinkerers long before *Make* magazine was even a dream. As further chapters will explore, this shows that the ideas of the Maker Movement, and the maker ethos, should be part of a longer understanding of history, detached from STEM learning and American manufacturing, that should be considered in history museums for what it is.

A PLACE FOR MAKING: MAKERSPACES AND HACKERSPACES

As Mark Hatch identifies in his *The Maker Movement Manifesto*, a makerspace is "a center or workspace where like-minded people get together to make things."[11] Intrinsically, then, the Maker Movement occurs in a place where the process of making occurs. These spaces are known by a wide variety of names, including hackerspaces, fab labs, coworking spaces, and innovation centers. These spaces for making can occur in a variety of different places, such as specialty located facilities (both public and private), schools, museums, and science centers.

A makerspace is one of the basic locational units of the Maker Movement. It is a place that is set aside for the process of making. The makerspace is an important factor in this book, and addressing how to bring the makerspace (and the Maker Movement) to the history museum will be a part of later chapters. Here are some basic components of what make a makerspace a makerspace, at least in the sense of the Maker Movement thus far:

- A makerspace is a place where people can use technology (which could be anything from digital technology to more traditional technology) to make things. A makerspace is not solely confined to new technology: it can include anything.
- A makerspace is a tangible place, set aside for people to make things.
- A makerspace is a place where a community can make together. A makerspace is a place to learn and grow together as a community.
- A makerspace is a place that encourages critical thinking and the use of technology to solve problems.
- A makerspace is a place where makers can share what they have made with the group, as well as share their skills.

There are other forms of makerspaces, but many build off the ideas mentioned above. Sometimes, this can lead to greater specificity. For example, a hacklab is a space that is reliant on technology. At its most basic, a hacklab is a place that offers open access to computers and the internet. Often, these very computer systems are created and built by makers. They include refurbished, recycled, or custom-made machines. Likewise, many of the systems run on open-source platforms like GNU/Linux.[12]

An essential element of the Maker Movement is that it is connected to the idea of community. Community requires a sense of place. That place is the makerspace, or whatever other name is given to it. For the sake of this book, with its focus on making outside of digital technologies, "makerspace" will be the word used to describe the collaborative physical place where making occurs.

CRITIQUES OF THE MAKER MOVEMENT

The Maker Movement has problems: first, the Maker Movement's triumphalist approach to the utopian promise of capitalism, technology, and production; second, the Maker Movement's focus on technology in the face of other, less "plugged in" forms of making and expression; and finally, and most importantly, the Maker Movement's marginalization of voices who are non-white, non-male, those with disabilities, and those experiencing economic disadvantages. These three issues are intertwined, and build off of each other. Each is an important problem that the Maker Movement, if it is to be something that is a force for good in the world, needs to address. For each, in part, I will discuss the ways that historical making and historic sites can help answer some of these critiques.

They are important for anyone considering being part of the Maker Movement, and bringing the Maker Movement into your historic site, to consider. This should not be cause for choosing to not engage with the Maker Movement; rather, perhaps, makerspaces at historic sites can be part of the solution here.

THE TECHNOLOGICAL UTOPIA: MAKERSPACES, CAPITALISM, AND PRODUCTION

One of the grand narratives of the Maker Movement is the idea that it represents a turning point, that it is a shift into a new industrial revolution, as proposed by Chris Anderson,[13] or, according to Mark Hatch, that it is a revolution.[14] Anderson and Hatch are but two individuals, but their texts about the Maker Movement are some of the most widely cited (and most often critiqued) texts regarding it. These narratives, of a new industrial revolution and of a revolution, are exceptionally triumphalist, and are centered around ideas such as the regaining of American manufacturing supremacy or the rise of industry itself.

Likewise, Mark Hatch's revolutionary rhetoric is very much tied to stressing the importance of his own company, the now defunct TechShop.[15] The revolution that Hatch describes is powerful: it is the rejiggering of manufacturing and aims to create a manufacturing world in which the worker has more access to the means of production; in other words, the world can be made better by the egalitarian access of equipment in a makerspace.

Both Hatch's and Anderson's conceptualizations are strong ideals, but they are also unrealistic utopian thinking. The Maker Movement is powerful, and can very much be a part of the ways in which manufacturing changes in the digital world, the ways in which people can access information and learn new skills, and the ways in which it can lead to the formation of community. It would be naïve, though, to think that these triumphalist narratives of the Maker Movement are not connected to or in service of capitalism. While there is much to be said about the open-source nature of the Maker Movement as a force for good, a revolution in the market it is not. As Debbie Chachra has noted, "Making is not a rebel movement, scrappy individuals going up against the system . . . while the shift might be from the corporate to the individual (supported, mind, by a different set of companies selling a different set of things), it mostly re-inscribes familiar values, in slightly different form: that artifacts are important, and people are not."[16]

CIRCUITS AND TECHNOLOGY: MAKING THE INTANGIBLE

The Maker Movement privileges certain forms of making over others. That is to say, it privileges technology such as electronics, robotics, 3-D printing, and computer-centered tools over other, more traditional (and unplugged) modes of making.

Part of the focus on technology could be because of Silicon Valley's desire to bolster the Maker Movement in schools, which leads to the development of new coders and others who use technology. The market (and the money) leads to a definition of what the Maker Movement is: in short, it becomes a movement that, despite its egalitarian promise, exists to support and bolster Silicon Valley.

As the previous history of the Maker Movement in this chapter has shown, the idea of a movement of making, and making in a community, is not new and has not always been confined to the digital world. In fact, making's connection to the digital world and digital fabrication is relatively new. This has been perfectly summed up by Josh Giesbrecht: "This is what bothers me when I see things like digital fabrication or robotics billed as the 'game changer,' or when I hear Leah Buechley asking why it is that nearly all of the projects in Make Magazine feature electronics, or robots, or Arduinos, or something else that Make Media will sell to you. These tools should be situated in a larger context of construction, architecture, mechanics, textiles, etc. Instead, we see them elevated to a high status because, as best as I can tell, they let programmers who've been lost in a world of material-less abstractions actually apply their skills to something physical, something real."[17] The Maker Movement, then, has fallen into the trap of the new: technology and innovation have become exciting in their own right, and the movement has centered around them. Rather than viewing technology and innovation as something that can inform the world around them, they have been elevated. It becomes all about technology.

This book, at its heart, is about advocating for the use of traditional tools and making methodologies as part of the Maker Movement. As a result, this critique is one of the main challenges of this book and will be addressed throughout the subsequent chapters. It's important to think, though, of the implications of the Maker Movement centering on new technology and innovation. In part, it makes the Maker Movement exciting and innovative: that is a good thing. But it also limits the voices of people who are traditionally marginalized in technology discourses.

We should then turn to the most important of critiques, which is that the Maker Movement marginalizes those who are not white, male, heteronormative, without disabilities, and are economically advantaged.

THE RICH WHITE BOYS CLUB: RACE, GENDER, AND CLASS AND THE MAKER MOVEMENT

One of the most concerning critiques of the Maker Movement is that it can skew to being a white male space in which women, people of color, disabled people, non-heterosexual people, and the economically disadvantaged are allowed less of a voice and experience barriers of entry. Essentially, the Maker Movement presents itself as the formation of a new world through technology and innovation, and through that rhetoric marginalizes people when it comes to discourses in the sciences. Moreover, it is for a specific class of people: the sort who can go to a Makerspace and tinker, and with that tinkering find a place to create and grow. In spaces like Anderson's new industrial revolution, which prides itself on the egalitarian access of materials, innovation, and technology, leveling the playing field and access to the means of production, that democratization is not for everyone. It is not for those with lower incomes who might not have the time or resources to learn at a makerspace or the ability to devote their time to becoming part of a maker community.

Lauren Britton notes that, while the Maker Movement has made overtures to being more inclusive, those movements "focus on transforming women, on areas that need to be corrected, such as raising confidence, creating more woman/girl friendly learning environments, increasing ability in math and science, and so on. The women themselves cause the problem; they lack confidence, they are unable to learn in the 'normal' STEM environment, they do not embrace their full capability in math and science. It is the women who are deficient."[18] This is very evident with publication choices that were made by Make Media in 2009. The organization, which publishes *Make* magazine, had also published a magazine called *Craft*, which focused on more traditional crafts and was skewed toward more artistic means of production, in favor of publishing solely under the maker banner as one single magazine; the end result, though, was the marginalization of discourses surrounding craft. As a result, the Maker Movement focuses on making that is deemed more "masculine," such as coding and technology, and minimizes making that is deemed more "feminine," such as craft. This critique has also been leveled by Debbie Chachra, an engineering professor, in her essay "Why I Am Not a Maker" mentioned previously. Chachra argues that the ways the Maker Movement centers the "cultural primacy of making, especially tech culture—that it is intrinsically superior to not-making, to repair, to analysis, and especially caregiving—is informed by the gendered history of who made things, and in particular, who made things that were shared in the world, not merely for hearth and home."[19]

This was further highlighted by an issue around the founding father of the Maker Movement, Dale Dougherty, and the Chinese DIY YouTube personality Naomi Wu in 2017. Wu amassed a large online following, but quickly online communities such as Reddit (an anonymous online forum community) began to debate if Wu was actually a maker or if she was an actor who was standing in for a male maker or a group of makers. As one post on Reddit noted, Wu was not the "tech genius she claims to be. She is a puppet that was created to garner views and free stuff for her engineer husband."[20] Though just one example, this post shows the main thrust of the discourse surrounding Wu: that she was too beautiful, too feminine, to be an actual maker of substance. Dougherty bought into these conspiratorial discourses, noting, in a deleted tweet, "I am questioning who she really is. Naomi is a persona, not a real person."[21] Shortly afterward, facing backlash from the online community and realizing that he was wrong, Dougherty published an apology on *Make*'s website, saying that it has always been the goal of *Make* "to be inclusive and provide an arena for all Makers to share their projects, values, challenges, and humanity in a safe and supportive environment. If we fail at that, we take it seriously. I failed on Sunday and learned a valuable lesson from all of you about that."[22] Dougherty's apology did not fix the problem of the Maker Movement's relationship with women, and the discussions around Wu revealed serious issues, many of which centered around the idea of the "fake geek girl," the idea that attractive women (or women in general) doing "geeky" things like attending comic conferences or learning to code are pretending, and that real women couldn't possibly do such things. Wu, a real maker, shows that this is nonsense.

From the way it has always been imagined and realized, then, the Maker Movement skews masculine, centers around masculine forms of making, and favors male makers over female ones. There has been a pattern (particularly centered around maker publications and online interactions) that favors ways of making and makers that are male and disregards ways of making that are feminine. As a result, while it might not be outwardly hostile to women, the Maker Movement seems to have been falling into long-held patriarchal traditions that marginalize female voices and disregard female work and expertise.

This same strategy, it seems, has been used by the Maker Movement when it comes to interacting with people of color. While progress has been made toward the inclusion of people of color in maker communities, there is still very much work to do. Just as the Maker Movement has skewed itself to privilege male voices, so, too, it privileges white voices. Michael Lorenzo Greene, Nadia Kellam, and Brooke Charac Coley explored the interaction of men of color and university makerspaces. They have discovered that those makerspaces reflect the dominant, primarily white, culture of the institution in which they are located and of engineering in general, and that this "challenged smooth navigation in and through the spaces" for men of color in particular.[23] In looking at this research and issues surrounding race in the makerspace, Jennifer Brown concludes that race, while it might be something that is talked about in makerspaces and in maker culture, is not something that is addressed with any urgency. A space is not created for makers of color, and discussions are not held about uncomfortable topics surrounding barriers of access to makerspaces for non-white groups.[24]

Finally, another critique when it comes to people is about privilege and access. As described by its proponents, the Maker Movement is all about egalitarian access of tools, equipment, and technology. Egalitarianism, though, is only an ideal. While the Maker Movement is ideally egalitarian, access to a makerspace, access to the equipment in a makerspace, access to technology in general, and the availability of time to learn skills in a makerspace are a privilege, and a privilege connected to class. As a result, the Maker Movement is not a movement for all, but rather a movement for some, for those who have the time to access the makerspace and to utilize its materials, and to learn its secrets. Further, there are problems of access for people with disabilities, who experience difficulties entering makerspaces that are configured for non-disabled people.

There are intrinsic problems of equality and privilege that are part of the genetics of the Maker Movement. As historic sites, we work to tell the stories of the marginalized in our interpretation and presentation of the site. As a result, we have the inherent knowledge that the world has been skewed against voices who are non-white and non-male. Likewise, the presentation of that story, which is exceptionally difficult to do, is being worked on by museums and historic sites.

One of the ways in which these issues can be addressed in the makerspace is stated by Jennifer Brown, that a critical approach should be used in understanding the ways in which the makerspace functions within the existing social problems of race, class, and gender. For Brown, the answer is not broad strokes, which are the easy solution. Rather, the makerspace should be a place where "explicit conversations" about accessibility, disparity, and social justice–related issues can occur.[25] The Maker Movement can be an important force for good in creating a space for people who have been, until now, marginalized within it. The difficult discussions must be had.

THE MAKER MOVEMENT AND HISTORY MUSEUMS

The Maker Movement has as much promise as it does problems. It is part of a long history of communal engagement with the processes of making and formation of group identity. Likewise, it is an inheritor of discourses that have been problematic, including the marginalization of individuals, triumphalist narratives, and focusing on some technologies over others.

The Maker Movement, with all of this considered, is a valuable addition to the world of the history museum. Subsequent chapters of this book will explain the ways in which the Maker Movement can (and should) be added to the world of history museums and historic sites. To make is a valuable way of encountering the past. The museum world has much to gain from taking part in the Maker Movement. Before opening a makerspace at a historic site, it is important to understand the Maker Movement, both where it comes from and the problems that are inherent in it. This leads to two assertions: First, the Maker Movement is something that can be a valuable part of history museum world. Second, the inclusion of makerspaces in history museums can actually, in some ways, address some of the problems of the Maker Movement.

WHY MAKERSPACES? WHY HISTORY MUSEUMS?

History museums have done hands-on demonstrations for generations. Candle dipping, drop-spindling, and blacksmithing have been processes that museumgoers have long encountered as part of their experiences. However, at least concertedly, the idea of making and makerspaces has taken root in science museums and science centers, but not in history museums.

The subsequent chapters will explore the ways in which the Maker Movement is something that should be a part of the world of the history museum. However, in considering the makerspace and the Maker Movement, it should be noted that:

- Making and the Maker Movement are not solely confined to the digital world. Making and processes have a long history. That history is already happening at historic sites and has been for generations.
- While the Maker Movement has its problems, the central tenets of the movement—egalitarian access to making, making in a community, and taking joy in the process—are important ways for people to interact with the idea of making and the historic site in general.
- The ideas of the Maker Movement can be used to bolster the ideas of the demonstration and living history, providing a more dynamic (and more modern) approach for people to interact with historic sites and historic making.

As the rest of this book will argue, making and the Maker Movement are natural partners to the world of the history museum and the world of historic making.

HOW CAN HISTORIC SITES HELP FIX THE MAKER MOVEMENT?

Museums and historic sites have been working toward creating spaces that are inclusive and that challenge established narratives, as well as change the ways in which people interact with their world around them. In order to be a viable movement, and a movement that is inclusive of all sorts of different makers, the Maker Movement has a lot to learn. While this book is primarily concerned with the role of the Maker Movement in historic sites, it is also evident that applying the Maker Movement to historic sites challenges some of the established problems of the movement, as well as possibly offering some potential solutions. This can happen in a variety of ways, but some could be found below:

- Museums and historic sites are doing important work to reach out to the communities that they serve. This includes people who are traditionally marginalized, as well as people who have been traditionally underserved by historic sites in the past.[26] This is important work: museums and historic sites, at least in the United States, have previously been a part of telling triumphalist narratives of American exceptionalism, which centered around white settler narratives, the narrative of American greatness, and the reverence of the past, which in part entered the stew of American museums around the time of the bicentennial. Likewise, museums have been elite spaces for generations, many of them forming as a way to edify the masses, to raise them from the darkness of their ignorance.[27] This is shifting to create a space for the joint formation of history and for the creation of a space to have difficult discussions.[28] While museums have an exceptionally long way to go in addressing problems in both society and within the museums themselves, the modern museum world has done much work toward that goal. It is telling that these same problems are found in critiques of the Maker Movement. With thoughtful application of maker methodologies to the world of historic sites, it seems possible that the work that museums and historic sites have done to address these concerns could help to alleviate them within the broader maker community as a whole.
- The historic makerspace, as this book will contend, is about learning a process and reveling in that process. It is not about profit, but rather about learning, growing, and experiencing. Certainly, those skills could be applied to economic endeavors. At its heart, though, the application of makerspaces to historic sites is not a revolution; rather it is an assertion that the process and the taking part in that process as a community are as important as the finished product.
- The historic makerspace is about tactility, about getting one's hands dirty in the past. While, certainly, digital technology could be used, it is about interacting with the past. Technology is wonderful, and we live in an amazing world constructed by and joined together by technology. Information and the world are at our fingertips. While it would be foolish to say that making that centers around technology is not important (it is very important), it is also exceptionally foolish to only focus on digital making rather than other, more traditional forms of making. As a result, the umbrella of who

is considered a maker (as proposed by publications such as the very tech-heavy *Make* magazine) is narrowed. In focusing on other forms of making, the historic makerspace advocates for the importance of more traditional, less plugged-in forms of making.

The inclusion of the makerspace and the Maker Movement is not a panacea. It will not solve all of the problems facing historic sites, nor will it solve all of the problems of the Maker Movement. Rather, broadening the idea of what the Maker Movement is, and having museums take part in that, can benefit, diversify, and grow both communities.

Next, this book will turn to the idea of the Maker Movement in the historic site and the ways in which it can benefit those historic sites.

NOTES

1. Mark Hatch, *The Maker Movement Manifesto* (New York and Chicago: McGraw Hill, 2014), 5.
2. Ibid., 6.
3. Chris Anderson, "20 Years of Wired: Maker Movement." WIRED UK, May 2, 2013. https://www.wired.co.uk/article/maker-movement.
4. "The 'Maker Movement' Creates D.I.Y. Revolution." *Christian Science Monitor*, July 6, 2014. https://www.csmonitor.com/Technology/2014/0706/The-maker-movement-creates-D.I.Y.-revolution.
5. Chris Anderson, *Makers: The New Industrial Revolution* (New York: Random House, 2012).
6. Wendy Kaplan, *The Arts and Crafts Movement in Europe and America: Design for the Modern World* (New York: Thames and Hudson, 2004).
7. Anna Kelsey-Sugg and Chris Bullock, "Men's Shed Expert Barry Golding Says Opening the Door to Women Could Ensure Sheds' Survival." ABC News, November 19, 2021. https://www.abc.net.au/news/2021-11-19/men-s-sheds-improving-diversity-to-ensure-they-survive/100609334.
8. "Men's Sheds: Australian Men's Shed Association: Find a Men's Shed." Australian Men's Shed Association, February 15, 2022. https://mensshed.org/.
9. Barry Golding, *The Men's Shed Movement: The Company of Men* (Champagne, IL: Common Ground Publishing, 2015).
10. Alan Watts et al., "Houseboat Summit," in the *San Francisco Oracle*, no. 7 (March 21, 1967).
11. Mark Hatch, *The Maker Movement Manifesto* (New York and Chicago: McGraw Hill, 2014).
12. "Hacklabs and Hackerspaces—Tracing Two Genealogies." Journal of Peer Production. Accessed February 19, 2022. http://peerproduction.net/issues/issue-2/peer-reviewed-papers/hacklabs-and-hackerspaces/.
13. The Maker Movement as a new industrial revolution has been most popularized by Chris Anderson, in *Makers: The New Industrial Revolution*.
14. Revolutionary terminology, including a very flawed reading of Marxist ideology, can be found in Mark Hatch, *The Maker Movement Manifesto*.

15. TechShop unexpectedly filed for bankruptcy in November 2017. See Dan Woods, "TechShop Closes Doors, Files Bankruptcy." Make, November 15, 2017. https://makezine.com/2017/11/15/techshop-closes-doors-files-bankruptcy/.
16. Debbie Chachra,. "Why I Am Not a Maker." The Atlantic. Atlantic Media Company, January 23, 2015. https://www.theatlantic.com/technology/archive/2015/01/why-i-am-not-a-maker/384767/.
17. Josh Giesbrecht, "Make, Make, Make, Make Makemakemakemake." _thoughtLost, December 1, 2014. https://www.thoughtlost.org/make-make-make-make-makemakemakemake/.
18. Lauren Britton, "Power, Access, Status: The Discourse of Race, Gender, and Class in the Maker Movement." Technology & Social Change Group, March 18, 2015. https://tascha.uw.edu/2015/03/power-access-status-the-discourse-of-race-gender-and-class-in-the-maker-movement/.
19. Chachra, "Why I Am Not a Maker."
20. Nicole Kobie, "How a DIY YouTuber Became the Target of a Sexist Conspiracy Theory." The Outline, November 9, 2017. https://theoutline.com/post/2459/how-a-diy-youtuber-became-the-target-of-a-sexist-conspiracy-theory?zd=1&zi=4ngs7xmz.
21. Ibid.
22. "Dale Doughtery, Makezine." Makezine:Internet Archive, November 2017. https://archive.org/details/Makezine?sort=-date.
23. Michael Lorenzo Greene, Nadia Kellam, and Brooke Charac Coley, "Black Men in the Making: Engaging Maker Spaces Promotes Agency and Identity for Black Males in Engineering," The Collaborative Network for Engineering and Computing Diversity, Washington, DC: American Society for Engineering Education, April 14–17. https://www.asee.org/public/conferences/148/papers/24991/view, 2.
24. Jennifer Brown, "Critical Race Theory and Makerspaces: A Practical Approach," in Maggie Melo and Jennifer T. Nichols, eds., Re-Making the Library Makerspace: Critical Theories, Reflections, and Practices, 11–26 (Sacramento: Library Juice Press, 2020).
25. Jennifer Brown, "Critical Race Theory and Makerspaces: A Practical Approach," in Melo and Nichols, eds., Re-Making the Library Makerspace: Critical Theories, Reflections, and Practices, 24.
26. See, among others, Alexandra Olivares and Jaclyn Piatak, "Exhibiting Inclusion: An Examination of Race, Ethnicity, and Museum Participation," Voluntas: International Journal of Voluntary and Nonprofit Organizations (2021); Kayak K. Murray-Johnson, "From the Inside Out: Museum Educators and Professional Development on Race Talk," Canadian Journal for the Study of Adult Education 31 (2019): 129–38; Kerry Downey, "Reaching Out, Reaching In: Museum Educators and Radical Transformation," Journal of Museum Education 4 (2020): 375–88; Melanie A. Adams, "Deconstructing Systems of Bias in the Museum Field Using Critical Race Theory," Journal of Museum Education 42 (2017): 290–95; Jason Porter and Sydney S. Garcia, "Learning from Doing: The Evolution of a Dialogue-Based Program About Race," Journal of Museum Education 43 (2018): 291–98; Radiah Harper and Keonna Hendrick, "Doing the Work: A Discussion on Visioning and Realizing Racial Equality in Museums," Journal of Museum Education 42 (2017): 163–68.

27. See, particularly, Edward P. Alexander and Mary Alexander, *Museums in Motion: An Introduction to the History and Functions of Museums* (Lanham, MD: Altamira Press, 2007).
28. The literature here is broad, but some great sources include Hilde S. Hein, *The Museum in Transition: A Philosophical Perspective* (Washington, DC: Smithsonian Books, 2000); Kathryn E. Wilson, "Crafting Community-Based Museum Experiences: Process, Pedagogy, and Performance," *Journal of Museum Education* 24, no. 3 (Fall 1999): 3–6; Nina Simon, *The Participatory Museum* (Santa Cruz, CA: Museum 2.0, 2010); Amy K. Levin and Joshua G. Adair, *Defining Memory: Local Museums and the Construction of History in America's Changing Communities* (Lanham, MD: Rowman & Littlefield, 2017).

2

History and the Maker Movement

From the spinning wheel to the book-binding workshop, historic sites have long used the idea of making and hands-on activities as a tool for interacting with the past. Much of this making at historic sites has been going on before the Maker Movement was realized as a conceptual reality in the early 2000s. The hands-on activity is just part of the genetics of the ways that history museums have engaged with the public. If we apply the ideas (and ideals) of the Maker Movement to making in the history museum, we can move toward a more meaningful understanding of what it means to make, what it means to make to interact with the past, and what the museum means in the modern world and in the modern community.

In this chapter, we are going to explore the ways that the Maker Movement can be a part of the world of history by taking the ideas of the Maker Movement and incorporating them into the processes, hopes, and goals of history organizations. The result is the use of historical processes and methods in the context of a makerspace: historical making. Historical making can be used at historic sites to make them more dynamic and to help form community. It can be used as a tool and framework for improving living history. Historical making calls for democratization of historical information and the creation of community dialogues about the past and the present.

THE MAKER MOVEMENT AT HISTORIC SITES

The Maker Movement is a powerful ethos that historic sites can foster and adapt to engage with making, with the idea of being a maker, with a community of makers, and to learn to interact with new technologies. At its ideal, it represents a democratization of access to materials, the ability to learn to use those materials, and the ability to use those materials to make new and exciting things. As the previous chapter has shown, while there is much promise, the Maker Movement also should be questioned and challenged, as it is entrenched in issues of sexism, ableism, classism, and racism. These are major problems and challenges that should be confronted by both the Maker Movement and the historic sites that employ the maker ethos.

There is, perhaps, no better example of the Maker Movement at a historic site than the Eli Whitney Museum and Workshop, located in New Haven, Connecticut. The site was the location of the workshop that was employed by Eli Whitney, the inventor of the cotton gin. The Eli Whitney has integrated the idea of making into the very fabric of the organization, which runs workshops, programming, and an extremely successful apprenticeship program, in which children between the ages of 13 and 18 take part in a multiyear program, where they learn vital skills not only as makers, but also as part of a team. Making at the Eli Whitney is not connected to historic trades, necessarily. Rather, it is connected to learning valuable skills, most especially, valuable, tactile skills. As Ryan Paxton, executive director of the Eli Whitney Museum and Workshop, and Andrew Sargent, the site historian and lead educator, explained in an interview, this program and focus on making have turned the space into a dynamic workshop, where the entirety of the site is used and interacted with. The site literally comes to life. The site is "a museum, but not what you would expect."[1] One of the elements of my discussion with Ryan and Andrew that is particularly important is their insistence that what happens at the Eli Whitney is separated from the ideas of the Maker Movement. For them, the Maker Movement can be more focused on quick results, rather than on the honing of a craft. Making at the Eli Whitney is focused on the long game: on learning, on broadening and widening skills, on the broader educational idea of learning how to make something. This example can be exceptionally helpful as we bring making into the historic site. It takes the ideas of the Maker Movement and connects them to something deeper and more meaningful, something closer to what historic making looked like when people practiced these historic trades and crafts as their profession and as their livelihood.

Engaging with the Maker Movement at a historic site is far more than making a thing. It is the embrace of an ethos and the possibilities of that ethos—and what that ethos can do for our sites and our visitors. In a way, historic sites are one of the originating places of the maker ethos; it's time we embraced it again. Let's use it to make new possibilities and new ways to engage our communities.

WE'VE ALREADY BEEN MAKING

Making has long been a part of historic sites through demonstrations, through workshops, and to aid interpretation behind the scenes. Visitors are familiar with the idea of experiencing something being made, or even with learning how to make those things themselves. At sites such as Colonial Williamsburg, visitors can experience a wide variety of trades skillfully re-created by historic tradespeople. At historic house sites throughout the country, a visitor might experience someone cooking on a hearth or spinning wool. Other historic sites might offer the opportunity to learn a colonial craft through work-shops or special presentations. Some historic sites might be employing the making of materials, such as the sewing of historical clothing or the making of reproduction materials, to help with their interpretation. Making has long been a part of the world of history museums, historic sites, and living history.

Some examples of hands-on programming that many historic sites are already doing include:

- Workshops for the learning of a particular skill. Usually these workshops are one-day events, where participants learn a skill and complete an item. Sometimes this can be a multiday project as well. The goal of many work-shops is both to teach the craft and to produce a finished item.
- Learning a historic trade for children, usually in the context of a school trip or children's event.
- A historic trade or craft that is demonstrated or actively practiced for a museum-going audience. This is a major difference that can be found at places such as Colonial Williamsburg. As textile historian and former interpreter at the milliner shop at Colonial Williamsburg Sarah Woodyard noted, demonstration of a craft means showing the process from start to finish. People actively practicing a craft are working as if the shop was still functioning and visitors may see any part of the process of making but not the whole process.[2] In both of these examples, visitors are an audience to the making and witness someone doing the making; they can, of course, engage the maker and ask questions about the process.
- A making project at the museum, where museum staff, volunteers, or in-terpreters are learning to make something to aid in the interpretation of the site. Some examples of what this could look like are hearth cooking, sewing garments for first-person interpreters to wear, or tending a kitchen garden.

These are just a sampling of the ways that the idea of making something has been used at historic sites prior to the Maker Movement. The programs described above are helpful and meaningful and provide an excellent way for historic sites to engage their visitors. They are tried-and-true methods for en-gaging the public and interpreting historic sites.

These traditional making programs can be broken into two camps: First, they can be programs where the finished object is the goal; such programs are heavily led by a workshop leader. In this scenario, a group of people (children or adults) is brought together at a certain time and led through the making of something to a finished product. Often, the goal of programs like this is to intro-duce museumgoers to the ideas and concepts of making in a controlled setting, where, in an appointed amount of time, people learn about a trade or craft and then do it. Often in this situation, the work is guided by a workshop leader, who will guide the group step-by-step through the process of making something from point A to point B, along a predetermined track of making.

Second, many of the ways in which making occurs at historic sites is through demonstration, where people watch a craft being done but might not get their hands dirty themselves. A visitor can encounter someone doing the work and may interact with them. Often, that maker appears in historic clothing and will interact with visitors in first or third person, providing context and background to what they are doing and answering questions about the work. This can be within the context of an event, as an event itself, or as part of a regular experience at a historic site. Either way, what is key is that in this scenario visitors do not take part in any making; rather, they witness the making occurring and have some level of interaction with the person who is doing the making.

These are valid ways of interpreting the process of historic crafts as well as engaging the museum-going public with the idea of making and the concept of being a maker. However, they represent only one facet of what making means in the context of a historic site. There is so much more potential. In these contexts, making can be static, can focus on one interaction, is more focused on the museum professional or interpreter, and does not provide much of a space for the visitor to encounter, question, and grow. They focus on the presentation of a historic skill as a performative act or focus on the finished product of a workshop, rather than a trade as lived or a process as learned. With this, museums have missed the point about what making can be. They view making as transactional, and as the finished product. A shift in perspective is needed. In order to engage the public, ourselves, and the past we are interpreting, it is pivotal to understand the learning and teaching of a historic trade as not a finished product. Rather, it was a skill that was honed, tinkered with, adapted, and changed over time. When we teach a group of people to make one basket, focus on the process of getting them from step 1, a pile of reeds, to step 12, a finished basket, we miss the point entirely. We must consider those other steps in between: the process, the learning, the trade as it would have been lived by the people who used it. We need to focus on making itself.

A lot can change when we shift the view and think about making as something that is a process rather than an end goal, when we think of possibilities rather than following one route to the finish line. A lot can change when we as historic sites engage the Maker Movement.

BRINGING THE PAST TO LIFE BY MAKING

Based on how museums and historic sites already interact with the public, the Maker Movement is not a break from the ways that making has been a part of the world of history. It is an acknowledgment of what hands-on history can be and the potentials for reimagining the historic site. It presents both a framework for understanding the idea of making as a deliberate and meaningful act, as well as a pedagogical understanding of what it means to make (for more on a pedagogy of making in museums, see the next chapter).

Rather, applying the Maker Movement to the work of historic sites is a shift from the ways that making occurs at historic sites into new territory.

In thinking about the Maker Movement, broadly, and how it defines itself and its goals, we should consider the many facets and threads that it has across different applications:

- *The Maker Movement is collaborative and open sourced.* At its ideal, the Maker Movement is meant to be just that, a movement: it encourages people working together in groups, accomplishing tasks as a group and collaborating to solve problems together. The Maker Movement has an emphasis on the idea of open-sourced knowledge: this is most readily applied to open-source software and open-access to technology; it can also apply to ideas and processes. Information on making, in the ideal, is shared with the group rather than kept secret and proprietary.
- *The Maker Movement focuses on the process of making.* While makers are keen to complete a finished product (who isn't?), the finished product is not always the most important part. Rather, the focus is placed on the process, on the road that one took to go from idea to completed product, on the techniques and skills used. In a way, this emphasizes ideas and processes as the valuable product rather than the finished item itself.
- *The Maker Movement is about exploration.* The Maker Movement is about tinkering. In that vein, it is also about the acceptance of failure in the process of making. Modern understandings of what it means to make outside of the Maker Movement focus on the success of the finished product and can ignore the painful processes of trial and error, success and failure, that form the basis of what it means to make something.

These three ideas have nothing to do with emergent digital technologies which have become intrinsically tied to the Maker Movement as we know it today. They have everything to do with the idea of making and what it means to be a maker. It is here, in the desire for collaboration, for process, and for exploration, that the ideas and ideals of the Maker Movement can be applied to the world of history museums in the best sense.

In later chapters, we will explore the idea of a pedagogy of historical making (chapter 3) and how to set up a historical makerspace (chapter 4). One of the trends of the Maker Movement is to define the movement as revolutionary. Mark Hatch organized his *The Maker Movement Manifesto* as a manifesto, as a call to action for a new movement for a new industrial revolution.[3] The idea of a manifesto can be somewhat overblown and can skew the ways in which we think about what is being manifested in it. However, it also provides a concise and easily referenced guide to the call to action. I do not believe that the Historic Maker Movement is an answer to all the problems in the fields of museums, historic sites, and history in general. But I do believe it is a step in the right direction.

Historical making can help revitalize historic sites and forge the process of making into a meaningful activity that helps build community around the museum itself. That revitalization needs to be concise, understandable, and meaningful; it needs a guide and a call to action. In this spirit, I would like to propose a Historic Making Manifesto. It is made in the spirit and ethos of the Maker Movement's grand ideas and the movement's hope for dynamic possibility.

Make it your own.

HISTORIC MAKING MANIFESTO

Getting one's hands dirty is an important way to learn how people in the past lived and encountered the world around them. It provides a place where people can find empathy with those who lived in the past and who live with us in the present, united across time and space by the human desire to make something.

It is a powerful way for people to experience museums today.

Historical making builds off the successes of the Maker Movement and applies them to understanding the processes of making in the past, using the very modern and digital ideas of the Maker Movement and the makerspace to understanding and encountering history. Historical making understands and acknowledges the problems inherent in the Maker Movement (such as sexism, racism, classism, and an over-focusing on capitalist outcomes), as well as the challenges of the museum field and the world of history, and works toward solving them through human interaction.

This Historical Making Manifesto is divided into six statements about historical making. As you apply the ideas of historical making and embrace the ethos of the Maker Movement, feel free to add ideas to your own Historic Making Manifesto, in the style of the open-source ideals of the Maker Movement.

- *Historical making is for everyone.* A historic makerspace is an inclusive space, as a museum should be. Everyone should be welcome at a historic makerspace and historic makerspaces should be built with minority or underrepresented groups in mind, allowing a space for people of different backgrounds, perspectives, and abilities to come together and form community. A historic makerspace is open to all and professionals who work within a historic makerspace should work toward eliminating barriers of entry into historic sites and museums. Everyone is welcome and everyone is welcome to make together. The Historic Maker Movement is not a wholesale solution for all of the problems of the Maker Movement, the history museum, or history in general, but it can help lead to the formation of communities that can work to solve those problems in a compassionate, equitable, and mindful way.

- *Historical making provides a safe place to learn and grow.* An important element of the Historic Maker Movement is that it provides a place for people to learn about the past by making, learning to make, and learning the joy of making. In this is the acknowledgment that learning to make is a practice, and a practice that often does not bring immediate success. In learning to make, failure is more common than success, and many failures have to happen to reach even a semblance of mastery. They are key to learning. The historic makerspace, then, is a place where learning is encouraged, successes are celebrated, and failures are embraced as the learning experiences they are. While not everyone that encounters a historic makerspace or the Historic Makerspace Movement is going to start making things according to historic methodologies outside of the historic makerspace, their interaction with it can help them gain an appreciation for what human hands can do and encourage them to make something themselves.
- *Historical making is collaborative.* Making is not something that should be done in a vacuum, nor is it something that should be done in a very closely orchestrated setting. While a workshop moderator is an important element for teaching new skills and encouraging and challenging makers, the goal of a historic makerspace is to foster a community where making occurs. Resources should be shared, information on how to do things should be shared, research should be shared. The past does not belong to one person, and neither do the processes of the past. By fostering an environment of open-sourced information about the past and the processes of the past, the historic makerspace stresses that history is for everyone.
- *Historical making is about humanity.* When we learn to make, we learn about ourselves. We become a member of a group of people around the world who make things. Humans have been making things since we first evolved into a distinct species. To make is something that is inherently human. When we make and when we are mindful of making, we are not only forming a culture of makers but forming a culture of people who appreciate other humans both living in the world today and living in the past. When we learn a historic trade, it allows us to encounter makers of the past, to encounter the things they created, and to give voice to people whom history has made voiceless. By making, we gain empathy, both for people living in the world today and for the people who lived in the past.
- *Historical making keeps the past alive.* Skills and trades can become endangered: the things people make and the things people use change over time as the world around them changes. Museums are places where the past is preserved for generations to come. When a historic trade is learned in a museum and a museum becomes a place where historic making occurs, historic processes and technologies are preserved in the same ways that

historical collections are preserved. They become a way for us to learn about the past and to learn about ourselves.

- *Historical making is a research tool.* Historical making is more than a tool for visitor engagement. Rather, it is a powerful research tool for learning about the ways in which things were made in the past and the ways that material culture shaped the world.

The Historic Making Manifesto is broad and philosophical and might border on the idealistic, but it is also important for the ways that making can be incorporated into the idea of the history museum and the world of history. Trends across the Historic Making Manifesto focus on the role of the museum and historic site in the community, in providing a diverse space for everyone; in providing a safe space to learn, grow, collaborate, and listen together; and providing a space to think about making as an important tool for understanding the past. These are ideals, but they are within easy reach. They are also tenants that museums and historic sites should take to heart.

However, the world is not based on a philosophical ideal, and sometimes more concrete questions need to be answered. This is especially important when the idea of a historic makerspace must be sold to an organization's board of trustees, management, or stakeholders.

Outside of the statements above, here are some additional thoughts on how the historical maker is a vital and viable consideration for historic sites:

- The Historic Making Movement provides for the formation of community within a historic site, which can lead to new community involvement, new connections in the community, and new stakeholders, which will in turn improve the positioning of the site within the broader patchwork of the community of which it is a part.
- The Historic Making Movement encourages diversity, and provides a way for the museum or historic site to interact with communities of people who might not have previously felt that they were being served by their local community museum.
- The Historic Making Movement provides a new and dynamic series of programmatic offerings which can be aligned to a museum's mission, vision, and strategic plan.
- A historic makerspace and engagement with the Historic Making Movement can lead to greater visitation, as well as repeat visitors to the site. This leads to more eyes in the museum, the spreading of word-of-mouth advertising about the organization (the cheapest and best form of advertising), as well as increased income in the museum and gift shop.

The Historic Making Movement is a revitalizing force that can reenergize museums and historic sites. Rather than encountering a site that is static and noninteractive, visitors to a site that embraces the Historic Making Movement encounter a place where the past comes to life, where they can interact with the processes and materials of the past and ask new questions about the past as a community of makers (or, at the very least, a community of people who can touch things).

The idea of the Historic Making Movement is very aligned with current trends in the field of history, including Franklin Vagnone and Deborah Ryan's *Anarchist's Guide to Historic House Museums*[4] and Nina Simon's *The Participatory Museum*.[5] Vagone, Ryan, and Simon argue that historic sites (and museums, in general) must consider their audience and community, and move away from the idea of the preciousness of encountering the museum. In short, they argue that museums and historic sites need to get off their high horses and present history to the community in ways that encourage community engagement with history and with the historic site.

In the modern world, museums are no longer the bringer of information from on high, no longer the undisputed guardian of the past, a knowledge palace of the Enlightenment. Museum professionals and historians still have the important goal of preserving the past, caring for the objects in their collection, and ensuring that the stories of the past are told in accessible and meaningful ways. However, modern museum-going audiences are less interested in being spoken at, and are certainly less interested in taking part in a boring, static house tour ("look at this chair here . . ."); instead, museum visitors of today want to interact with the past, to experience and learn new things in ways that challenge and excite them. They want an experience. They want to form new ideas. They want something that they cannot experience somewhere else. As museum professionals, we can deride that and say that we know better, or we can accept that and accept the excitement that comes with it. Historical making is an acceptance and embrace of these new ideas and experiences.

The Historic Making Movement is a powerful addition to the arsenal of history museums. It can provide new, dynamic ways of engaging with the past and with the museum's community. Likewise, it can be a benefit to the museum itself, creating new community relevance, new interest in the organization, and new revenue streams. On both a philosophical and a practical level, the idea of incorporating the Maker Movement into the world of the history museum makes an enormous amount of sense.

Then we must turn our attention to the other way in which people interact with the past: through reenactment and through living history.

THE MAKER MOVEMENT AND LIVING HISTORY

Living history is one of the main ways that people experience the past on a daily basis at historic sites. It has a long history as being part of the world of the historic site. Likewise, it is one of the more exciting ways that people encounter the past.

Living history is a performance in which an individual or group of individuals dress in the clothes of the past and attempt to re-create a historical moment as best they can for an audience. Sometimes this can be a specific moment (such as the reading of the Declaration of Independence) or it can be a broader moment (Williamsburg, Virginia, before the American Revolution). As part of this, individuals can do an impression or representation of an actual individual (Benjamin Franklin in the 1770s or Mark Twain after publishing *Huckleberry Finn*). Sometimes, individuals will interact with visitors in the first person, talking about how they specifically did something ("I took part in the Continental Congress"), or sometimes in the third person ("Benjamin Franklin would have done this . . .") or sometimes a combination of both. Sometimes this can skew toward the awkward (questions regarding those strange talking boxes that people are carrying around with them), alienating (people might be not inclined to ask questions because they feel they could ruin the performance), or confrontational (in which visitors attempt to stump the historic person). Living history is a powerful tool for engaging the public, but it, like anything in the field of history, has problems. Many of these problems have been noticed by theater historian Scott Magelssen, who notes that while performance is an important way to engage people in the past, it can also provide a barrier for engagement.[6] Magelssen sees a way around this, though, and advocates for the idea of a second-person interpretation, in which visitors have "more agency in determining the trajectory of their encounter with history."[7]

In order to assess the ways in which the Maker Movement can be applied to the field of living history, it is important to ask what living history is and what it can do. Some could argue that it is a performance, and that by engaging the audience in that performance a shared communal narrative can be created.[8] Scholars of historical performance like Alevtina Naumova see living history as the creation of an environment, which she notes: "my discussion of a living history museum space implies the intersection between multiple senses—tactile, auditory, visual, and that of taste—in understanding the 'sensory sphere' constructed by a living museums space."[9] Living history experiences are carefully constructed and curated spaces in which the organization presents a tactile experience of the past to encourage visitors to ask new questions of the past. Current scholarship and questions about living history stress a movement away from the static performance in most contexts, and, instead, suggest that living history experiences should be just that: an experience. Visitors and interpreters can interact with the past, ask questions of each other, and engage themselves in new and compelling ways.

Making has long been a part of the field of living history. Much of what we know about historic trades and crafts and their practice has come out of the world of living history, which includes a plethora of talented interpreters who interpret trades and crafts (some of which have been interviewed for this book), as well as people who create materials and goods for living history interpreters to engage with, to wear, and to use. Making and living history is intrinsically tied: one could not exist without the other. Living history forms a basis for understanding the past and allowing craftsmen to work with methods that are as close to the past as possible. Historical making provides the necessary equipage for the interpretation of the past by living historians. While sites that might engage in historical making might not necessarily also use living history interpretive strategies, it is important to understand the deep connections that already exist between them.

Bringing the Maker Movement into living history eliminates the barrier between the living history interpreter and the audience of visitors. It allows the visitors to take part in the historical moment, to encounter the past for themselves, and to ask questions about the past. Rather than experiencing an interaction in which one interpreter has to set the entirety of the scene, making and living history allows for the group to work together to interpret the past.

Of course, this still will require the expertise of a living history interpreter, who is able to guide the group, ask questions, and help them achieve what they would like to achieve. But in this context, the living history interpreter becomes more a facilitator, guide, and part of the group rather than the educator or the person with the authority. The application of the Maker Movement to living history allows for living history to be pushed in new and compelling ways. Here are some examples:

- If a group of people learns a historic trade together, and may be working together, it can create the experience of a community of people who might be working together in a trade shop or other similar environment. The group of makers in a makerspace can work together to learn not only about the trade that they are accomplishing but the world in which that trade was done: Who were the people impacted by the trade? What sorts of trade routes and larger movements were needed? What was it like to work as part of a group in making an object?
- In breaking down the barrier between the performer and the audience, making can become a tool for group interaction and for group interpretation. This is close to what Magelssen advocates for, in that it is aimed toward giving the museum-going public a space to perform together, and a space to get off of the pre-established track of the performance. Making, the confines of making, and the physical realities of making can provide an important framework and background to allow for second-person interpretation.
- Making being incorporated into living history brings living history into the modern era. It provides a place where people can interact with the past, as well as with the present and each other. Further, it allows a space where play is permitted and where questions are encouraged. Rather than history being a performative act, making and living history allows for collaboration.

- Making and living history allows for museums, interpreters, and guests to interact with under-documented individuals and groups from the past, which allows for the assembled group to question broader narratives and helps to give a voice to the voiceless.

Making and living history is far more than taking part in a historic trade. Likewise, it is far more than giving a museumgoer tools and telling them to have at it and make a thing. Instead, it is the application and combination of two distinct ideas: that of making and that of performance. Rather than just going through the motions of the past, or participating in a sort of historical pantomime, making allows individuals (both visitors and interpreters) to physically touch the past, to think about the materiality of the past, and to ask questions about what that means, both for the past and for the present.

IF YOU LOVE IT, LET IT GO: MUSEUMS, POWER, AND MAKING

Museums were created to be a place where a learned group of people—curators and historians—educated the public out of the darkness of their ignorance through giving them "truth." Thankfully, this conceptualization of the function of a museum is falling by the wayside, as museums work to make themselves places where the community can come together and have difficult conversations, where narratives can be questioned and systems of power can be revealed and challenged. They have moved from showing the past as one unquestioned timeline of historical progress to providing several timelines and questioning why some timelines do not include certain events. More importantly, the world of the museum has moved into one where experts work alongside the community to tell the community's collective story with, not at, the community.

Bringing the Maker Movement into history museums and historic sites is one more step in this process. In calling for history to be collaborative, tactile, and done by the group rather than presented by the one, the idea of the Maker Movement decentralizes the role of museum staff and the historian with a capital H. Instead, everyone can become a historian and everyone can become a maker. This is exciting, but this is also scary: What if they get it wrong? What if something terrible happens? What if they misunderstand?

In bringing the Maker Movement into the history museum, a museum professional is accepting a wide variety of things. First, that they will be creating a space where people can learn and make together in a collaborative way. Second, that that making is something that will be done by the group. Third, that a historic makerspace is a powerful tool for inclusion and the creation of community. Finally, the makerspace and the idea of historical making is an important way to learn about the past. Most importantly, a museum professional will gain a new understanding of what being a museum professional is. Essentially: they become a collaborative expert.

What does it mean to be a collaborative expert? In the Maker Movement, both outside and inside the world of the history museum, there are experts. Experts help keep learners on track, and help ground what is being done in known and existing knowledge. Likewise, experts know how to ask questions, know what questions to ask, and know where answers might be found. In a museum experience with a traditional workshop, an expert leads the workshop and guides the makers through each individual step, checking on them as they go. In a museum experience with an emphasis in the Historic Making Movement, an expert will provide guidance on how to do the work, will talk about how we know what we know, and then will provide a place where people can make. The expert becomes less a central person teaching a workshop and more a guide, who can provide background and expertise, as well as real-time feedback. The work of learning, troubleshooting, failing, and problem solving falls on the people who are doing the making. To be a collaborative expert, the museum professional should work to decentralize themselves from the experience as much as possible. They are the guide, and they are with people along for the ride. They should be open about their own challenges and failings, and help to encourage the challenges and failings of other makers. They, too, should ask questions and interrogate the past.

This can seem scary and daunting from the view of a museum professional. Essentially, the Historic Making Movement brings with it a level of uncertainty. Will the group fail? Will people come to understand the goals of the project? Will they be able to draw conclusions about the past? With a guide who is concerned about collaboration and community, rather than their own ego, they most certainly will.

This is also scary because it decentralizes the narrative of the museum. Rather than being a place where a carefully curated story is told to a viewership, in the context of somewhere like a historic makerspace that narrative can be questioned and interrogated by the group. Of course, experts can be helpful here, to prod, to question, and to guide. But this should be more exciting than not. Many museums are interested in bringing new members of the community into their doors: minorities, the all-elusive millennial (of which I am one), and underserved communities. The historical makerspace allows a space for those new constituencies to experience, to learn, to grow, to form community, and to question the established hierarchies of history and the idea of the museum itself. This is far more powerful than just trying to get new people through the doors or creating specialty events for new constituencies. It provides a place for people to come together and to form that community, together. It also provides a warm place that truly shows that the organization is interested in being a part of the community—not just a place where people in the community go sometimes, but a vital place where the community comes together and knows itself.

But what does it mean to be a maker? What does it mean to learn about history through making? In the next chapter, we will explore the pedagogy of making as it relates to museums and history.

NOTES

1. Ryan and Andrew generously sat down and talked at length about the site, its programs, its philosophy of making, and the ways in which that making interacts with the general history of the site. Ryan Paxton and Andrew Sargent, personal interview conducted on September 21, 2022.
2. Interview with Sarah Woodyard, March 2, 2022.
3. Mark Hatch, *The Maker Movement Manifesto* (New York and Chicago: McGraw Hill, 2014).
4. Franklin D. Vagnone and Deborah E. Ryan, *Anarchist's Guide to Historic House Museums* (London and New York: Routledge, 2016).
5. Nina Simon, *The Participatory Museum* (Santa Cruz, CA: Museum 2.0, 2010).
6. Scott Magelssen, *Living History: Undoing History through Performance* (Lanham, MD: Scarecrow Press, 2007), 146–50.
7. Scott Magelssen, "Making History in the Second Person: Post-touristic Considerations for Living History Interpretation," *Theatre Journal* 58 (2006): 291. Magelssen argues here that second-person interpretation can go very far; it could include allowing museum visitors to embody famous historical personages and to experience historical events with all of their contingency and opportunity. It's a powerful and compelling argument.
8. Stephen Gapps, "Museums of the Living Dead: Performance, Body, and Memory at Living History Museums," *Journal of Curatorial Studies* 7 (2018): 248–70.
9. Alevtina Naumova, "'Touching' the Past: Investigating Lived Experiences of Heritage in Living History Museums," *International Journal of the Inclusive Museum* 7 (2015): 1–8.

3

A Pedagogy of Museum Making

What does it mean to make? Some might say it is to combine things to make a new thing. But, as we set out to make historic makerspaces at museums and historic sites, we need to be aware of what it means to make on a deeper level. We need to be aware of what it means to educate and to learn. We need to think about making as a pedagogy.

This chapter explores making as an educational experience and works toward finding a pedagogical framework through which to understand and better facilitate the makerspace experience for learners and makers of all ages.

While historical making can be applied to a wide variety of pedagogical strands, this chapter will seek to understand making through a pedagogy known as constructivism. This approach centers the experience of the learner, or, for us, the maker. Constructivist pedagogy questions more traditional assumptions about what a museum is and how the public interacts with it. Discussions of pedagogy can be thick, dense, and theoretical. The mention of theory might make it tempting to flip to the next chapter. I encourage you not to. It is important to understand the theory of learning by making, what it means to learn and question the world through making things with one's hands, to make makerspaces that provide a space for meaningful experiences.

JUST WHAT IS PEDAGOGY ANYWAY?

For many historians and museum professionals, outside of academia, education, or museum education, pedagogy might be a foreign concept. Essentially, pedagogy is a way to understand teaching and a way to understand how different learners react to different educational processes. To study pedagogy is to study different methods of teaching and engaging with learners.

Pedagogy is often broken up into five different approaches which focus on various educational strategies. The five different pedagogical approaches are:

- Collaborative: Learners work together and aid each other in learning. Often, they learn in small groups.
- Inquiry-based: Students address problems by asking questions and doing further research. Often, this is connected to real-world problems and real-world solutions.
- Integrative: Students engage in cross-disciplinary education, bringing together traditionally separate disciplines to gain a deeper understanding of whatever they are studying.
- Reflective: Students and teachers reflect on their lessons and assignments to improve the educational experience.
- Constructivist: Learners are involved in the learning process; they create their own meaning through the material rather than by passively receiving information. Learners make meaning and knowledge.[1]

The reality of any sort of educational process is made through the skillful interweaving of these pedagogical frameworks. Thinking about making as a pedagogy will rely on thinking about the intersection of many of these different pedagogical frameworks: rarely is it all just one.

This chapter is primarily concerned with the last of these pedagogical concerns, a constructivist approach. I think it is the one that makes the most sense for working with makers in this context. Likewise, constructivist pedagogical theory has long been a part of the ways museum educators view their work. Working and learning in a constructivist sense is ideally suited to the idea of the makerspace. Any approach to education, in a museum or otherwise, will include an intertwined collection of these pedagogical theories: they build off of each other and organically intertwine into a full educational experience. We will be talking about museum education in the context of the historic makerspace, which relies on creating meaning and knowledge. A makerspace also relies on collaboration, on asking questions and solving problems, on working across disciplines and across time, as well as reflecting on the process and the practice of making itself.

If we are to consider constructivism as an important lens through which to view the makerspace, we should be aware that this lens will assume the following:

- Knowledge is made. Knowledge is not engrained, nor is it received through passive absorption: the learner creates knowledge and experience.
- Learning is something that occurs as a process that is active. People learn by doing, not by sitting and receiving information. Learning is a continual practice; it is a contact sport.
- Learning and gaining knowledge is part of the social experience of being human. Learning happens as a shared practice in the context of a social environment. This environment can occur in person or it can be a com-

munity or culture of learning which creates a body of knowledge through shared experience.

- An educator is a facilitator rather than an instructor. Educators provide the context for learning, as well as aid and guide learners to facilitate the process of learning. But they do not act as the lone instructor. An educator provides helpful knowledge and backup for learners, who are stepping out of their comfort zone and into the unknown, as well as makes adjustments and changes depending on the experience of the learners.

These ideas are applicable to many contexts in which this pedagogical framework is applied. It is particularly helpful in understanding the ways in which a makerspace could function from an educational standpoint. It shows that it should be a space where education and the development of knowledge is something that is done by the group through the experiences of the makers rather than an imposed narrative. Any staff in a makerspace should see themselves as facilitators and guides rather than as instructors.

Let us now take these ideas and apply them to the world of museum education, and, more broadly, the role of the museum in contemporary society.

MUSEUM EDUCATION AND CONSTRUCTIVIST THINKING

Constructivist pedagogy has long been tied to museum education, often taking the form of engaging the audience with the work of museum interpretation, where a group dialogue formed through open-ended questions and exploration can help the group generate new knowledge and new ways of looking.[2] Knowledge is created through a shared dialogue between learners and teachers, who form their own experiences making meaning in the gallery, with a focus on the autonomy and perspective of the student through the guidance of the educator.[3]

Art museums are an exceptional lens through which to view a constructivist methodology at work. Throughout the mid-twentieth century, many museums introduced studio-based programming, where students would learn about the artworks in museum collections through making artworks based on the techniques used by artists in the collection.[4] By making artworks based on the techniques of the past, students will gain a deeper appreciation of the artworks they encounter in the gallery, and will cease to see them as static pieces hanging on a wall; instead, they will see them as documents from the past, which allows for them to ask new questions about the artwork, the people that made it, the time period it came from, and the broader world of which it was a part.

This thread of museum education should also be seen as part of broader shifts occurring in museums. Rather than viewing a museum as a place where knowledge is given and questioned, museums are becoming a place where communities can come together and make meaning. This shift, from imposed knowledge to the communal generations of knowledge, is one of the genetic traits that could lead to the creation of dynamic public engagement, programming that involves the community, and the makerspace. This shift informs the ways in which visitors interact with museums and interact with living history professionals (see chapter 2).

These shifts are also part of modern trends toward decolonizing the museum and making the museum a more accessible and meaningful place for the entire community. The modern museum is formed through the intersection of many fields and exhibitionary strategies, to the point that it becomes difficult to define what the modern museum is, which leads to discussions of the post-museum. The post-modern museum seeks to challenge preconceptions of the museum.[5] For scholars like Eilean Hooper-Greenhill, who coined the term "post-museum," the post museum is a solution to the problem of modern museums which are grounded in nineteenth-century understandings of education and knowledge production. She views the post-museum as a place based on the transmission of information. Information is the main approach, and the post-museum "can be analyzed by understanding communication as an integral part of culture as a whole."[6] Advocates of the post-museum are less interested in transferring knowledge and more interested in engaging the public with culture and inspiring discussion and reflection among the group, aiming for the generation of new knowledge.[7] The post-museum as a concept is intrinsically tied to the idea of constructivist pedagogy. Rather than viewing the museum as a space where information is given, constructivist teaching (and, thereby, the post-museum) views the museum space as a place where knowledge is generated in the form of a group.

This discussion of the post-museum might seem too theoretical for some: What does that have to do with the on-the-ground realities of actual life in the trenches in a historic site? While it could easily be dismissed as some scholarly scribblings, the concept of the post-museum has major implications for the ways in which historic sites, as well as the programming we do there, interact with the community in which the museum is located and the people within that community.

As museum professionals living in the modern world, one of the major concerns we can have is creating a space in our museums that is accessible, friendly, and welcoming of the diversity of our communities and the communities of people that our museum serves. Likewise, we as a profession are moving toward telling more complicated narratives of the past, in which we question established narratives, many of which have been based on constructions of power. As we move toward creating a space that is welcoming of diversity, we need to be aware of what a museum is, inherently, in its genetics. When we do that, and when we come to grips with it, we can work toward understanding the history of the museum and what the museum means for people who encounter it.

The museum is an inherently colonial act. When museums first became something that existed, it was as a way for governments to display and claim possession of the lands and peoples that they had colonized. The Spanish Empire displayed materials from their American colonies as a way to show that they owned those colonies.[8] Likewise, the British, through collections such as the British Museum, created a visual encyclopedia of colonialism.[9] These ideas were not confined to Europe, nor were they confined to the more distant past. As museums were formed throughout the United States, they were geared toward telling tales of American exceptionalism, Manifest Destiny, and the inevitability of American greatness. These ideas crystallized with the formation of museums surrounding bicentennial celebrations in 1976, in which the national narratives of the founding fathers, Betsy Ross, the scrappy ingenuity of American colonies, and the vanishing nature of indigenous America were crystallized into national reality. Folk heroes like Daniel Boone became national heroes, when, in reality, they worked to colonize lands that were already lived in by indigenous Americans, marginalizing the continent's first inhabitants from the national story and the national way of life. Many historic sites are still grappling with this historic past of the world of American museums. In my own personal experience, smaller historic sites walk a fine line between providing relevance to a world and working with the legacies of both the eighteenth century and the crystallized (and cleaned up and sensationalized) narrative of the bicentennial. When American museology crystallized as a field, we were telling the stories of the "great men" of history, the founding fathers who helped build the nation. Today we are moving toward the telling of more truthful, more complex, and more critical narratives. This is important work, and work that we must do in order to remain relevant in the modern world.

The way we present information matters. In these traditional narratives of the museum, information was presented from on high and was unquestioned by a museum-going audience, who accepted the stories of the past. In part, this is because the museum was viewed as a place where information was given: the museum is the expert and the producer of knowledge, and the people who encounter the museum are its unquestioning object.

In the modern world, these narratives are rightly questioned.

If we are to consider the traditional museum as an inherently colonial act, the post-museum is an effort to undo the museum's violent past. While the museum had always been a place for the giving of information, the post-museum centers the collective generation of knowledge. Knowledge is not imposed, the people who encounter the knowledge are given license to interact with knowledge and to generate knowledge. They are given access to knowledge and ownership of that knowledge. The community helps form knowledge together. Rather than an enlightened authority giving knowledge to the masses, the museum becomes a place where knowledge can be generated. Information belongs to all and is formed by all, even those traditionally marginalized by the museum and academia.

While constructivist pedagogy might be something as deeply theoretical as the idea of the post-museum, it is an important consideration for museum education and the idea of the modern museum. In a constructivist theory for encountering the museum, museum visitors encounter the museum and work to form their own narratives. Museum educators work to guide the visitors, as do museum programming specialists and museum curators (in a small museum, this collection could be the same person). Rather than one person giving knowledge (as in a lecture), a constructivist approach allows for the group to experience it, for the forming of collaborative human experiences, as well as the generation of new knowledge together.

These theories taken into the real world can help guide the field of museums in a new direction which is more equitable, more meaningful, and less colonized than the museums of the past.

MAKING TO LEARN: THE MAKERSPACE AND MUSEUM EDUCATION

Decolonizing the museum and considering the post-museum is an important goal for our field to be working toward. If we are to consider the makerspace as an educational tool, we must consider how it fits into existing discussions of museum education, which also means that we should consider it a part of the discourse to make museums for everyone, not just for some.

The makerspace is a learning environment. It is a learning environment in which learning is made through hands-on making and through collaboration with other makers in the space. Makers in a makerspace share ideas and processes, work as part of a team, distribute information, and work together toward common goals.[10] While there might be a facilitator of the activity or someone who acts as the educator, for the most part information is generated by the collective group, who work together to implement new strategies and problem-solving techniques. Essentially, the idea of the ways in which learning occurs in a makerspace falls into what we would consider to be constructivist theory. Makers make meaning and generate knowledge together.

The environment in which making occurs is incredibly important. We can understand the environment both as the environment of the museum itself, which provides a context and setting for the processes of making, but we can also understand the environment as the emotional and educational space in which the making and learning occurs.

Part of the work here, too, is reliant on the creation of existing ways of understanding and activating previously understood knowledge. In the context of museum education, this would mean things such as pre-visit information, providing context for the museum before students encounter the museum, as well as preparing students for the eventual realities of the makerspace and what they will encounter there. With this in mind, learners will encounter the museum and the makerspace as a place where they can explore, be invited to make assertions and take chances, and to make mistakes. They will be armed with the tools to understand what they are doing as well as what is being asked of them, which, in the case of the historic makerspace, is to explore and generate knowledge in a collaborative environment. This can be done through conceptualizations of the makerspace as the third teacher, made popular by the Italian educator Loris Malaguzzi. Malaguzzi noted that the makerspace joined the other two teachers (family and classroom teachers) and provided a place where children can express themselves in safety, learning and growing together.[11] Learning becomes social, and becomes ingrained and enmeshed with the idea of play.[12]

Much of the work surrounding makerspaces and education has been done through analyzing children within the maker environment. As a result, it might be difficult to talk about adult makers within the context of museum education. However, it is important to assert that while they are very different learners, many of the successes of making for children can be applied to adults. While we can address adults as very different learners, they most certainly can benefit from accessing the museum through a constructivist lens, through encountering and questioning the narratives of the museum, and through making as a way of generating new knowledge within a collaborative setting.

If we are to consider the historic makerspace within a pedagogical framework, we should consider the following when we are working toward creating our spaces:

- The historic makerspace is the creation of a space in which makers work together to construct new narratives of the past, of the museum, and of the objects they encounter there.
- The historic makerspace is a place where historic processes are learned, decoded, and developed. In this context, makers learn about the past from themselves, each other, and facilitators. This allows for the group to learn about the past.
- While making and the makerspace can be problematic (see chapter 1), the historic makerspace can, in the right context, provide a place for the questioning of established narratives about the past and about museums, as well as for the generation of new narratives. It can allow for an educational space where new and marginalized voices are given an important seat at the table.
- The facilitator or educator who works in the historic makerspace should be careful to not over-direct makers. It is important that makers have the skills and abilities to make the project. Likewise, it is important that they understand what the project is and have resources to succeed in that project. Finally, they should have someone who is available to ensure the safety of those working in the space. The facilitator or educator should see

themselves as a maker in the space as well, rather than as an educator who is giving information. They are part of the process, and should work to make sure that the space is collaborative and safe for all.
- The historic makerspace should be concerned about the environment of the place. It should incorporate and add to the educational experience of the museum and provide a space for new narratives to be developed.

The historic makerspace, then, should be a place where makers work together to generate knowledge about the past in a collaborative and constructive environment. Experimentation should be encouraged, as should the questioning of narratives and the formation of new strategies for understanding the past.

MEASURING SUCCESS IN THE HISTORIC MAKERSPACE

While the idea of the historic makerspace could be an exciting addition to museum education and museum programming, it is important to also consider what success means for the educational outcomes of the makerspace.

In part, success is based on the metrics and goals which have been established for the program as an educational source, which are dependent on the goals, visions, and outcomes that each museum sets for itself.

In the context of the museum, learners are not (and should not be) assessed through the testing of knowledge. A useful tool, though, could be something like Success Case Method (SCM), as popularized by Robert Brinkeroff. The Success Case Method can be used to analyze a wide variety of things outside of educational outcomes, but in this sort of context it would analyze the performance of the makerspace by looking at successes and failures that occurred within it. It involves identifying the program that is being evaluated, surveying for successes and challenges, interviewing successful cases, and creating recommendations.[13] Some questions that could be asked of the makerspace, in order to assess its efficacy, would include:

- The first series of questions could be demographic: How many people used the makerspace? How many of them were return visitors? How many of them had successful outcomes? What were the ages of the people who used the makerspaces? What were their gender identities? Demographic information? These questions provide a sort of census of makerspace users, and would provide important hard data for the ways in which the makerspace worked within the context of the museum.
- The next set of questions could be related to the context in which people use the makerspace. Are individuals taking part in the use of the makerspace through a regular tour of the site? Is it a program? Is it a school tour? Is this your museum or historic site's regular cohort of makers? (Many of these questions are dependent on the role that the makerspace has at your

historic site and the ways it is integrated into the site itself; see the next chapter.)
- The next set of questions could be related to the maker projects themselves. What sorts of projects are people making? What are the outcomes of those projects? What did people learn? Did they feel like it was successful? What did success look like for people in the makerspace? What would they like the makerspace to be?
- Another set of questions could be about the formation of a community in the makerspace. How are people using the makerspace? How are they interacting with each other?
- Finally, another set of questions could be about the perceived impact of the makerspace for both museum staff and for makers in the space. What is the value of the makerspace? What does success look like for makers? For facilitators? For educators? What does the makerspace provide the historic site that other things did not?

Some of these questions are open ended and some of them are more data driven. Some of them are more centered on information about users, others about the ways those users interact with the space and each other, and still others about the ways in which the historic makerspace interacts with the site and the community.

A good assessment of the makerspace as educational experience will address many of the above questions, but the questions being asked will depend on the site, the goals of the site, and the particularities of the space itself. It will also depend on the ways in which the makerspace is used: regularly or during programs, sometimes or always.

This data can be collected in a variety of ways, but for the effectiveness of the data, it is important that it be collected in ways that are consistent and that document the realities of the makerspace. In collecting data, it is always important to consider the interaction with the public. I once was somewhere on vacation and was asked if I would like to take a survey about my experience. I said yes, expecting it to be a quick survey (and, honestly, to be given a coupon or discount for my trouble). The survey ended up being an uncomfortable length of time, and no coupon was given. Data is important, but the time and patience of the person being asked for the data should be considered. Here are some ways in which data can be collected for the makerspace:

- No one but the people collecting surveys really like surveys, but they are an impactful and effective way of collecting information about user experience. Surveys can look like all sorts of things, be they paper or digital, but consider making them as unobtrusive as possible. Ask meaningful questions, but ask the questions that you feel are most impactful for your assessing of the makerspace.

- Provide an anonymous comment box, where makerspace users can provide anonymous feedback of their experience. Read and consider the comments (and have a thick skin about it: anonymous feedback can, at times, be brutal, but can also be insightful).
- Provide a space for facilitators and educators in the makerspace to provide feedback. This could look something like a specially constructed survey or a meeting.
- In the collaborative spirit of the makerspace, if you have a cohort of people who work in the makerspace regularly or even if you just have people working in the makerspace together, you can provide a space for collaborative assessment and for group discussion of performance. This could look like a group critique of work and process, or it could look like a facilitated discussion after a maker session.

Any organization's interactions with the community are based on data that assesses the impact of the organization and the ways in which the organization allocates resources. Data can be used both to measure the effectiveness of educational programming, in this case the makerspace, and to make the case to an organization's board of trustees that a continued investment in the makerspace is a valuable thing to do (for more on trustees and investment in the makerspace, see the next chapter).

This chapter has taken educational theory and made a case for understanding the makerspace through that lens. It has also shown that this way of thinking can complicate the idea of the museum and make it more equitable and meaningful for all. We have also looked at the ways that a makerspace can be assessed. All this theory considered, let us move to the more practical: let's make a historic makerspace.

NOTES

1. Arthur Guil-An, "5 Pedagogical Approaches in Teaching," Academia.edu, February 18, 2018. https://www.academia.edu/35955322/5_Pedagogical_Approaches_in_Teaching.
2. Juyoung Yoo, "Bridging Art Viewing and Making: Constructivist Museum Tour and Workshop Programmes," *International Journal of Education through Art* 17 (2021): 374.
3. Ibid., 375.
4. Ibid., 375–76.
5. Eileen Hooper-Greenhill, *Museums and Education: Purpose, Pedagogy, Performance* (London and New York: Routledge, 2007), 1.
6. Ibid., 125.
7. Sophie Jess, "Please Touch: An Exploration of the Bloch Building as a Post-Museum in the Nelson-Atkins Museum of Art," *Lucrena* 14 (2020): 63.
8. Tim Betz, "Better Than Seeing Fairy Tales: Contextualizing Curation in the Iberian Atlantic," *Hemisphere: Journal of Visual Culture in the Americas* 10 (2007).

9. James Delbourgo, *Collecting the World: Hans Sloane and the Origins of the British Museum* (Cambridge: Belknap Press, 2019).

10. Marco Braga and Gustavo Guttman, "The Knowledge Networks in a Makerspace: The Topologies of Collaboration," *International Journal of Science and Mathematics Education* 17 (2019): 514.

11. Nandita Gurjar, "The Italian Makerspace," *Childhood Education* (97): 49.

12. Ibid., 51.

13. "Making Progress: Evaluating the Success of Your Makerspace," K12 Blueprint. Accessed April 3, 2022. https://www.k12blueprint.com/sites/default/sites /default/files/PD_Resources_Schools.pdf.

4

Making a Makerspace in Four (Somewhat Easy) Steps

Hopefully by now you're thinking that a makerspace might be a good addition to your museum or historic site. After discussing the Maker Movement and how it can transform the field of public history, now is the time to take all that maker theory and apply it to the tangible, messy reality of your historic site. This is a complicated process that is individual to any historic site. This chapter provides a helpful and practical framework of the things that can (and should) arise as you set out to bring your makerspace to life. Rather than providing a one-size-fits-all template for making a makerspace, this chapter provides an adaptable road map that any historic site can use to help guide the messy process of making a makerspace.

A makerspace is an investment in your site and a shift in the ways in which your organization interacts with the public. Rather than just providing guided tours or program experiences, a makerspace shows a continued willingness to engage the public in new and meaningful ways. It also shows that your site is willing to relinquish some control and allow for guests to form their own experiences through making, in which your site is a facilitator. Moreover, making a makerspace is an assertion that you and your site care about teaching the public through hands-on processes of making. This is not just a financial investment (though we will get to that), but also an investment of time (both your staff's and in your site's calendar), an allocation of important physical space on your site, and important real estate space in your social media and messaging to the public.

In order to make the making of a makerspace somewhat digestible, this chapter breaks the process into four steps: Asking, Funding, Locating, and Maintaining. These steps will guide you through the important questions you, your staff, and your site's stakeholders should be asking as you set out to make a makerspace, such as: Why should our site have a makerspace? Who will pay for the makerspace? Where will the makerspace be located? Who will take care of the makerspace and allow it to flourish? What problems, challenges, and struggles will we encounter along the way and how will we overcome them? These important questions should be considered in depth before beginning. Let's start asking them!

ASKING

Before moving into more practical and tangible steps, it's important to think about how a makerspace will fit into the particular ecosystem that is your museum or historic site. Every site is different, has its own story to tell, and has its own history of interacting with the public. Maybe you have been part of your organization for a while and know much of this history. Maybe you are new to your site; it would be a good idea to learn about the history of the site and its community from old hands, volunteers, or the dusty (and often forgotten) spaces of your organization's files. It is important to know the unique ecosystem of your museum or historic site before you begin to consider a makerspace at all. You should know your organization before you consider making a massive change that would include a commitment like a makerspace.

Regardless of organizational history, many sites can benefit from the dynamism of the makerspace. Gather a team of people involved at your site and brainstorm about the idea of a makerspace and how it will be an addition to the life of your site and the interaction your site has with the public. This team should include a wide variety of people who intimately know your site: yourself, those involved in programming, volunteers, and organizational stakeholders. This group could include the people who I will later call your makerspace cohort, or it might not. In these early stages, it is important to bring together voices who know the organization and who are willing to experiment, and who will keep the discussion inside the organization for now (your makerspace will have outside friends soon enough!). Now is the time to ask yourself and your team some important questions about your makerspace and your organization. The first question you should be asking is "why do we want a makerspace?" It is one thing to know that makerspaces and making is a valuable part of the history museum and can be a transformative way for museums and history professionals to engage the public, but it is another to consider why one would work particularly well at your site.

Your site's mission and vision are exceedingly important. They are also the vital first test that the idea of a makerspace should pass through. As Harold Skramstad and Susan Skramstad note in their essay "Mission and Vision Again? What's the Big Deal?" as part of the Small Museum ToolKit series, a shared understanding of the purpose of the organization (the mission) and the ways in which that organization sets and achieves its goals (vision) is key to the continued successful operation of the organization and ensures that the organization itself continues on the proper track.[1] Mission and vision are vital to the organization's existence both in the present and in the future, and are key to keeping your organization, its stakeholders, its staff, and its messaging on brand and on track.

The idea of making and the makerspace should be read against and in concert with your mission statement and the vision that your organization has set out for itself. Missions and visions are as diverse and unique as historic sites themselves and it is impossible to say that certain conditions in your mission statement or vision indicate that a makerspace should be part of your museum's programmatic offerings. Assessing the makerspace against your organization's mission and vision, then, is not an "if this, then that." If only it were so cut and dried and simple! It is instead a question about how your organization sees itself and the ways in which a makerspace can help your organization meet its goals and increase its interaction with the community. Here are some possible scenarios that might show that a makerspace is right for your site:

Your site has a history connected to making

Many historic sites have a history that is deeply intertwined with the idea of manufacturing or making something tangible. Your historic site could be an old grist mill that once ground wheat into animal feed or an old farmstead that once housed families of cloth makers, as the sites I have worked at are. Or your site could have been an industrial factory which once employed people who made goods to be sold on a local, regional, or global scale. Or perhaps it was the home of someone who made their money off the goods that they sold and produced, which allowed for the house to be built and maintained and, eventually, for your museum to exist. How was the building, location, or infrastructure of your site created into tangible reality? It was made by the hand of a maker at some point. Having a history at your site that connects to the idea of making is a powerful way to show that the makerspace is a vital part of how your organization sees itself and educates the public about its history. It is one thing to tell visitors about the process of weaving that would have occurred at your site to help them understand the history of the place. It is another thing to demonstrate the process of weaving for them: "Ah, so that is how a loom works!" It's a totally different thing to have them sit at the loom and have them use the shuttle themselves. When they do that, they are truly interacting with the past and truly experiencing your site as a dynamic place.

Your site has a history of making at events and special programs

While perhaps any site can be connected to the idea of making in one way or another, many sites bring with them more recent traditions of making that have been part of programs for years and have become important elements for a community to engage with. Maybe your site has had events such as quilt shows or candle dipping. Maybe you have a long-standing tradition of having a living history event such as a reenactment day. Perhaps you have hearth cooking at certain events, or have volunteers or staff members who demonstrate certain skills. Perhaps you have a blacksmith on-site and visitors can occasionally watch them pound metal in the forge. A makerspace is leaning into that identity and forming it into tangible reality. Essentially, the solidification of a makerspace at your site, especially where making has already been an important part of your organization's cultural identity, is a statement by your organization that making is an important part of what you do and an important language with which you want to speak to the community. Rather than simply offering demonstrations as your site has perhaps done in the past, the creation of a makerspace shows that your site is a place where there is a commitment to dynamic making.

Your site has never done anything with hands-on making before

If your site has never done anything like this before, do not be discouraged. As has been described above, almost any site can be connected in some way to making. The history at any location in which a museum or historic site is located once had tangible material culture and was part of the tangible reality of lived human experience. In short: anything in the past can be connected to the idea of a maker in one way or another. Some sites might take more creativity than others to make a makerspace work, but it is possible almost anywhere.

You now might be able to organically position your makerspace within the broader architecture of your museum or historic site's identity, and you may have found ways in which the makerspace will be an important asset in interpreting your site and bringing your site's particular history alive for visitors in meaningful ways. The next step is organizational buy-in, which is as multifaceted and complex as any organization in and of itself; in part, we are talking about interpersonal dynamics.

An important first step is to ensure the staff who would be taking care of the makerspace are all on the same page about the makerspace and what it will be for the organization. They should have an idea about how the makerspace works alongside the organization's mission and vision, and how it complements existing offerings that the museum has. The idea of the makerspace should align itself, at least in part, with the organization's strategic plan. Likewise, there should be ideas about what the makerspace will be like when it is completed (see "Locating" below), and also a rough idea of how much the makerspace will cost, both to set up and to maintain. The next step is, perhaps, one of the most important. This is where your organization's board comes in (they may also be involved with funding, so more on that later). When configuring your site to be maker centered, it is important that stakeholders and the board of trustees, your overseeing body, are on board with the idea of the makerspace. Their support is vital to your organization and to what your organization offers to the public. Essentially, at the board level it is key that your organization has embraced the spirit of making as you set out on your journey to make a makerspace.

Here are some things to keep in mind as you approach, discuss, and recruit your board to approve the makerspace:

- Your board should be concerned about the general governance of your organization and maintaining your organization for the future. As a result, it is important to show that the makerspace is something that will be an ideal part of the organization, that it will help the organization engage with new parts of its community, will grow the number of stakeholders the museum has, and cultivate new donors and new relationships. The makerspace can be both an important programmatic addition to your museum as well as an excellent strategic step. Showing how the makerspace aligns with the organization's current strategic plan and institutional goals would be a good step here as well.
- While this book admittedly devotes many pages to talking about the philosophical and theoretical ideas behind a makerspace, these are things that are probably of less concern to your board at large. This is where your makerspace should begin to enter into tangible reality, and you need to have answers (with numbers and data) to the following questions: How much will it cost? How much time will it take? Who will work on it? What will likely be the return for us doing this? These may be less exciting questions for the historian, but they are pivotal in bringing your makerspace to life. It is important to remember that, at least in the case of governance, staff time equals money and the allocation of resources.
- Your board is one of the biggest advocates for your organization and could be one of the biggest advocates for your makerspace and the culture of making you are creating with it. Why not have a board retreat where you can show members the joy of making something to introduce them to the power of the makerspace? Why not regularly invite them to learn to make something with you? They might enjoy it, and it might offer them something different from their regular lives. As a result, they will probably talk to friends and networked associates about their experience. It is a net win for the museum and the makerspace, as well as for the community.

When meeting with the board, one should have ready the answers to all the practical questions of money, time, and resources. There should be a reasoned and well-articulated response (backed up by data, where available) that the makerspace will help the museum or historic site reach a new audience, strengthen an audience, and help it become a vital and dynamic part of the community. Such results can grow into important relationships for your museum, aiding it in reaching into new parts of the community, and, perhaps, cultivating a new crop of donors. A good course of attack could be to recruit your board into making themselves. Have them get their hands dirty, if they are willing. Choose a craft that is not too hard, not too easy, but also a little fun. Then let them make and experience!

Once your board is aligned with the idea of a makerspace, it is time to start expanding the idea into the wider community. This is the time to find your makerspace some friends.

Get the word out that your organization is taking steps toward creating a makerspace and try to find people who might be interested in being a part of it. This can help gauge community interest and find stakeholders who might be willing to participate on a physical or financial level. It can also give you an idea of the people who are local to your museum who might be interested in the makerspace and may help sustain it in the future. Here is just a sampling of those who might be willing to be friends with your organization and your makerspace:

- Your museum's existing volunteers, interns, or friends group
- People who have taken workshops at your museum in the past
- Reenactors, living history interpreters, or local historical experts
- Students and other interested learners of all ages
- Homeschool co-ops
- Families (many organizations have families who are regular visitors; they are a powerful and valuable resource to tap into)
- Individuals affiliated with other, non-history organizations, such as local arts organizations. It might be helpful to think of organizations that focus on making.
- Local artists, craftspeople, and those who make things with their hands. These people might not be historians, but they may be interested in making and creating something tangible already. Maybe they would be interested in challenging themselves with the art processes of the past?

There can be so many more! Reach out to the people in your community who may be important and valuable friends to you as you step out onto your organization's maker journey. They might have answers to questions about your community that you have, they might be able to help you troubleshoot specific problems, or they might be valuable ambassadors of your organization's maker-centered philosophy. Getting people involved will help make the makerspace (and your organization) a valuable part of your community.

Your makerspace is just about ready to shift from an unrealized dream to a tangible reality. You have figured out why your organization wants a maker-space and how it will interact with the organization as a whole, you have convinced your board to join you on your makerspace, and have found maker friends who will help make your makerspace. You have done the asking and the searching; now comes the making. With tangibility comes other lived realities of bringing that tangibility to life. With tangibility comes new challenges. Our discussion must now turn to the more practical concern of funding.

FUNDING

Funding your makerspace is vital to the process of creating one. Funding can break into two phases: initial start-up funding and continuous funding that sustains the makerspace on your site.

The start-up funds for a makerspace might be partially dependent on the existing infrastructure your historic site already has. Do you have a history of making at your site already? Maybe a closet (or basement, or attic) filled with craft materials? That can be, in part, a massive step toward the start-up of your makerspace. Ultimately, a first phase of a makerspace can be as simple as dedicating a folding table to your makerspace, posting about it on social media, and doing crafts there with materials you already have. Of course, it can easily spiral from there, and become something huge and expensive. A good step in thinking about funding and what you need to start the makerspace is to answer a series of questions: What materials do we have on-site for making right now? What materials do we need for making in a makerspace immediately? What crafts do we want to showcase there? The first is a practicality, and should be answered by doing an inventory of craft and program materials in storage. The second two are practical questions, but also reach back to thinking about what your makerspace is to your site. What do you want people to learn? What processes of making were important to your site or are readily seen in your site's collection? You might be curious as to what role existing infrastructure can have on the funding of your makerspace: it actually has a massive role. If your organization is already skewed toward doing programmatic offerings like workshops, you have existing infrastructure on hand that can be piped into the makerspace itself. You do not need to totally reinvent the wheel; just put a new hubcap on it. This eliminates start-up costs.

In an ideal world, your organization will always have a line item in its yearly budget to cover the funding of your makerspace and to invest in it as something that your organization does for the public. While that ideal world can be possible, it is important to also discuss and find avenues through which your makerspace could be funded, both at start-up and throughout its life. Here is a list of possible options:

- Local and regional granting organizations might be willing to fund the beginning of a makerspace, but they will also want to see their investment pay off in a sustainable way. A grant might be a good way to start your makerspace, but it is not a particularly feasible way to maintain your makerspace into the future.
- Your makerspace could be sponsored, either by a local business or individual, or by a combination of the two. Maybe, in identifying friends to your

makerspace and your organization, you found a patron or an organization that would be willing to fund the makerspace itself, and would be willing to commit to continued funding of the makerspace.

- The cost of your makerspace could be partially set off by having visitors pay a monetary fee for the use of perishable materials in the makerspace. Ways to do this could be the selling of project kits for use in the makerspace, or the outright selling of materials for use. With this, replenishment of materials would be paid for as they were used. A word of caution here: the charging of a set fee for the use of your makerspace could act as a barrier of entry to your makerspace, particularly for low-income or marginalized individuals. Some options here could include finding ways to offer reduced (or prepaid) materials through the support of a donor or a scholarship offered by your organization. Another option would be to have a pay-as-you-want model, in which users could pay what they feel they can afford for the use of the makerspace.

- Many museums and historic sites offer membership as a way of supporting the museum and granting perks for locals and frequent visitors. It is possible to tie the use of the makerspace to membership, and make it a perk of being a museum member, but that could make the use of the makerspace difficult for people who aren't members or do not have the resources of membership. It also can make the makerspace seem like an elite perk; in reality, the ethos of the makerspace is that it is open and available for everyone.

As you can see, there are a wide variety of ways in which your makerspace could be funded, both at its start-up and to keep it going. Now that your makerspace has been situated into your site and has been funded, it is time to think about the practicalities of bringing that makerspace into solid, tangible reality. First, it needs to be located on your site.

LOCATING

Where your makerspace will be situated in the physical reality of your site can help inform many of the other questions you and your organization might have as you set off on your makerspace journey. In part, location is everything. Also, location is nothing. A makerspace can be fantastically effective if it has its own delegated space within your museum, with walls and its own infrastructure. A makerspace can also be just as effective as a rolling cart that goes into a closet and comes out when it is needed. Or a folding table with boxes that are stored somewhere easily accessible. A makerspace is what you make it to be.

Part of what makes the makerspace such a beautiful concept for a historic site is that it is completely scalable and adaptable to your location: there is no one-size-fits-all makerspace. If your historic site is like any historic site I have ever been a part of, you do not have enough room. There is space, perhaps, but it is configured in strange ways that might have made sense in the 1800s (or the 1960s) but do not make sense for us today. Essentially, the first step in the makerspace and any making there is for the museum professional to make the makerspace work.

In locating where a makerspace is, you should define what a makerspace means for your site. One question to ask is, "Is the makerspace a place or an ethos?" Or perhaps, "What makes a makerspace a makerspace?" As we have previously explored, this answer is porous and changing depending on who tries to define it. For the sake of this book, I have chosen to define a makerspace as a place where people can interact together to make and to learn. It is an essential part of a makerspace that the making itself is communal. Watching someone make something is not a makerspace; it is a demonstration. The location for your makerspace can be whatever you want it to be, just as your makerspace should be what you want it to be and what works for your organization. However, a makerspace should include making and should also be in tangible reality. These are the intrinsic elements of a makerspace. The rest—the scale, the location, the portability, the storability, and more—is entirely up to you.

Want to try the makerspace and not dive right in? Dedicate a table to it in your gift shop or other part of your museum. You can also dive into something more solid and tangible, such as dedicating a classroom or gallery to the idea of making, forming a fixed makerspace. Only in your space and in your organization can you have any inkling of where a makerspace would go, but I have a hunch that somewhere on your site there is a space that is not too big but also not too small, where a table could be put and historic making could occur on a regular basis. You can imagine that place, too, can't you?

Then there is the question of time, which also helps in the locating of your makerspace. Your makerspace will be part of your organization, and can be accessible to visitors whenever you feel it is appropriate. As has been discussed at all points in preparing your makerspace, the situation of when that makerspace should be open to the public is variable depending on your organization. It is also variable depending on when you would like to fold the makerspace into your organization. In an ideal world, the makerspace would be open all the time, and would be an open-source location for people to come together and learn about the past whenever they would like to (or, more concretely, whenever the historic site is open). In the real world, this might not be something that is possible unless there is allocated staff who could oversee the makerspace on a daily basis. This is possible, of course, but is dependent on having a staff person who understands what the makerspace is and how it works, and who would be able to be a resource for people as they used the makerspace. Perhaps for your organization it would make more sense if your makerspace was open at certain times: perhaps on the weekend, when traffic around the site is more intense, or on a special making evening, or both. Time is the element most often forgotten about, but it tangibly places the makerspace within the usually clogged real estate of both your site's event calendar and the local community's event calendar.

There are additional challenges in bringing your makerspace to life that have to deal with its now imminent physical reality: lighting, sound, accessibility, safety, and storage.

LIGHTING

Lighting is an exceptionally important element of any makerspace. While the people of the past might have made things and tinkered under the light of candles or oil lamps, we now know that people work best with adequate lighting. The kind of lighting in your makerspace might depend on the permanence of the makerspace itself, but it would be prudent to have task lighting in addition to normal overhead lighting. Solutions that could work here include using already installed track light; installing new lighting, which could include overhead lights (either hardwired or plugged in); or bringing in movable lamps. Providing a well-lit makerspace will ensure that your makers will be able to see what it is they are doing within the makerspace.

SOUND

Sound is another element to consider. Your makerspace will have to fit into the physical reality of your museum, but it will also become part of the acoustic reality. The past was a loud place that included machinery, hammering, scraping, and assorted other noises which might be jarring to regular museumgoers (and also jarring to your staff, if they work in the same building as your makerspace). While the ideal might be to soundproof the makerspace, it could be helpful to lean into the acoustic reality of making within the confines of your historic site. Perhaps your site was a place where things were made originally; hammering and the use of tools could bring that place to life. Likewise, a makerspace that makes noise could also attract people to it, who are curious to find out what is happening there and eager to become a part of it. However, it is important to be aware of the possible negative effects that the sound of the makerspace could have on visitors, particularly for visitors who may be more sensitive to noise or have sensory processing difficulties. In the case of inclusion, then, it might be important to confine loud makerspace noises to a particular time, or to have particular advertised "quiet making times."

INCLUSIVITY OF ACCESS

Light and sound give way to another concern that should be addressed when you begin to bring your makerspace to tangible reality, which is that the makerspace should be inclusive of all members of the community. For reasons mentioned above, sound should be considered in a meaningful way. Also, the use of lighting can improve the makerspace and allow for greater access for the visually impaired. In addition to these environmental concerns, you should also consider the following:

- Is the makerspace located in a place that is accessible to a wide array of people from the community?
- Have we talked to people with disabilities or organizations that aid and advocate for people with disabilities in the creation of our makerspace?
- What is the experience of entering the area where the makerspace is located?
- Are pathways, entrances, and exits clearly marked and wheelchair accessible?
- Is the makerspace worked into other accessibility concerns connected to your site, such as access and inclusion?
- Are aisles, pathways, and hallways clear and free of debris, wires, or other potential trip hazards?
- Are there tools (such as scissors) for right- and left-handed people?
- Is printed information, including instructions, signage, and materials, available in a variety of formats? (This could include large print, braille, as well as instructional materials in different languages, depending on your local community's needs.)
- Are printed materials legible? Are materials printed in high-contrast, easy-to-read fonts?

Steps such as answering the above go a long way toward creating a makerspace that is inclusive of a wide variety of makers. They also go toward making sure that your makerspace is functional, accommodating, and safe for all who use it.

SAFETY

Safety is the most important element to consider in the creation of a makerspace. While many of the tools in a historical makerspace might be more analog than those in a more traditional makerspace (they probably won't include things like lasers or power tools—though they might!), they can be just as dangerous as modern tools and should be treated as tools rather than toys. Likewise, a historic makerspace can bring to bear a wide variety of materials outside of tools, including chemicals and substances, that are dangerous and should be handled with extreme care. This is a delicate balance. Makers should have a thorough understanding of the tools and materials they are using and the safety procedures that should be followed with them to ensure the safety of makerspace staff, volunteers, and the maker community. However, they should learn about safety in a way that does not scare them from the use of the tool. As with anything that is dangerous, from a car to a chain saw, safety must considered as mindful operation, respect for the tool itself, and knowledge of the tool and accompanying safety procedures. With this in mind, your museum makerspace should have:

- Safety procedures in place.
- A training program for teaching new makers about tools and materials that can be used in the makerspace. This training program should also include any staff or volunteers who will be involved in the makerspace.
- Clear and easily readable signage.
- Well-placed and clearly defined safety features, including exit signs and fire extinguishers.
- Safety gear, including gloves and safety goggles, and rules and regulations regarding their use.
- A makerspace code of conduct that includes guidelines for the use of tools and safety procedures. Ensure that those who use the makerspace acknowledge and follow this code of conduct.
- Procedures for maintaining and inspecting the makerspace. This includes cleaning and ensuring materials are properly stored, making sure that the aisles are free of trip hazards, and inspecting tools and equipment regularly to ensure safe operation.

Historically, many makers did not pay much heed to the realities of safety and the dangers of their work environment. It was simply a part of life. The modern historic makerspace, ensconced within your museum or historic site, should place safety as a priority. While we want our visitors to have a hands-on historical experience, we do not want them to have a hands-on historic medical emergency.

STORAGE

A final concern in moving to tangibility is the continued problem of storage, which is a bedeviling problem at any historical institution. Your makerspace's storage concerns are as unique as the organization that is going to house your makerspace. Here are some things to consider when it comes to storage:

- It is a good idea to be aware of the materials, tools, and supplies that your makerspace has, in part because it can cut down on operational costs and ensure the continued sustainable operation of the makerspace. A regular supply inventory is a good idea, and should be conducted at the very least quarterly, depending on the traffic that your makerspace receives.
- Unused and expired materials should be disposed of in proper ways and by following the proper ethical practices, including recycling and hazardous waste collections.

- Be mindful about the materials that are purchased for the makerspace. Be particularly mindful if materials can be used for multiple projects or if they have a shelf life.
- Do not be afraid to turn down donations of materials. Just because someone has a massive amount of fabric or yarn in their attic they want to get rid of (and that you might never use) does not mean you need to accept it for the possibility that it could be used someday in the distant future.

The actual method of storage will vary depending on your space and organization, and can include crates, open storage such as shelving (this is good because it lets people see the neat things you have; you just have to keep it neat and tidy), or a closet. What is most important when it comes to storage is that it is a functional system that works for you, your organization, and your makerspace, and that the system is followed by all users of the makerspace. Without a system, all the crates and shelving in the world won't matter and your makerspace storage will be a mess, which will hamper the functionality of the space.

With maintaining storage procedures in mind, let us now turn our discussion toward maintaining your makerspace.

MAINTAINING

A makerspace is like a car. Imagine when you got your first car, and everything was shiny and new (at least to you). Then you realized that cars are expensive, and you had to worry about replacing tires, oil changes, inspections, registration, and routine maintenance. Then you also need to fuel your vehicle. If these steps aren't done, your car will not run or you will get a ticket for driving without a registration. Getting a makerspace up and running is much the same. There is nothing more exciting than setting off on your makerspace journey: getting signage made, setting aside a table, placing materials into crates. So shiny and new! But then it becomes apparent that routine maintenance is necessary. Who will staff your makerspace and when? Who will be in charge of purchasing materials and ensuring that they are replenished and maintained? Who will be in charge of learning new trades and sharing them? The answers are individualized to your site. If you are the person coming up with the idea of the makerspace, many of these things might fall on you personally. Are you willing to take them on, in addition to your already overfilled to-do list? Maybe it's more of a team situation. If so, who will do what? Regardless of who takes part in your makerspace journey with you, it is important that you plan for the future of your makerspace.

Solving some of the problems voiced above could be divided into two groups of solutions. The first are issues that should be a part of the organization itself and should happen internally. The second are issues that can be addressed within the community that will be taking care of or using your makerspace.

Internally, some of the maintenance problems related to your makerspace can be taken care of by your team (or, if you're at a very small historic site, you). Many of the internal issues related to the makerspace—the staffing, the maintaining, the replenishment, and even the learning of new historic trades and crafts—can be solved through the creation of a schedule that monitors the rhythms of life in your makerspace and your organization, as well as the thoughtful allocation of duties across your makerspace team. In thinking about a team for your makerspace, include anyone on your staff who is interested, but especially people who oversee programs and education, as well as volunteers and interns. The rhythms of life in your makerspace, the needs of your organization, and the skills, willingness, and enthusiasm of your team are, of course, individual to your site.

Some of the other issues of maintaining the makerspace could be solved by the community that forms there. In their ideal space, a makerspace is inherently based on community and is inherently open source.[2] Forming a community is often easier said than done, but many times offerings at historic sites can be part of a community and have already formed a community around them: the regulars that attend events often are and have long been members of your site. Makerspaces and the process of making have a way of forming a community around them, especially within the context of historic making. With historic making, many individuals are attempting to make something they have never done before and are on a level playing field. As a result, a community can form through that vulnerability and shared experience. In forming a community of makers and cultivating that community, your makerspace will become something that your organization and the people involved with it can take pride in.

But what about the tangible problems of makerspace maintenance? Your community can help you keep the makerspace tidy and can help guide you along the way. Discovering new projects to attempt can be something that could be discussed with your maker community rather than thought up in a void. Curious about trying a new process? Maybe your maker cohort will be curious, too, and maybe you can experiment together. It's also very possible that someone who has gotten into historic making will want to learn something else, and will then want to teach it to the group. Teach someone how to tape loom and perhaps they'll go a step further and learn how to make bobbin lace. Making is something that humans evolved to do in a community. It only makes sense that the maintenance of makerspaces, the spaces where making is cultivated, occurs in a group as well. This is, of course, something that can't be manufactured; it must form organically. It is possible, though, and it is something that your organization should strive for.

Fostering a community of makers can also have an important effect on your organization, you, and the rest of your staff. A dedicated group of people who want to be at your makerspace will be energizing to the museum staff and will provide the necessary impetus to maintain the makerspace. It makes the entirety of the project worthwhile.

YOU'VE DONE IT!

Well, you haven't done it yet, and of course there is a lot more to do, but a makerspace is something that is tangible and possible at your site. Now it's time to get to work!

However, with all of this planning and site soul searching, there is an important point that I should make. A makerspace might not be for every museum or historic site. They represent a major shift in the ways in which an organization interacts with its public and engages them in the past. Moreover, they represent an enormous investment by an organization and a redefining of the ways in which your organization functions. Rather than shoehorning a makerspace into your museum or historic site and making it work, it is important that your site benefit from the inclusion of a makerspace. If you feel that your organization will not benefit from the inclusion of a permanent makerspace, don't fret! The Maker Movement is still something that you can bring to your site in other ways.

In the next chapter, we will explore the ways that the Maker Movement and the makerspace can be implemented in museum programming, interpretation, and exhibitions.

NOTES

1. Harold Skramstad and Susan Skramstad, "Mission and Vision Again? What's the Big Deal?" in Cinnamon Catlin-Legutko and Stacy Klingler, *The Small Museum Toolkit, Book 1: Leadership, Mission, and Governance* (Lanham, New York, Toronto, and Plymouth: AltaMira, 2012), 63.
2. For more on open-source makerspace initiatives, see Mark Hatch, *The Maker Movement Manifesto: Rules for Innovation in the New World of Crafters, Hackers, and Tinkerers* (New York: McGraw Hill, 2014), 104–6.

5

Putting the Makerspace to Work: Programming

Now that your site has a makerspace and has invested in creating a maker culture within that makerspace, it's time to put it to work. This chapter illustrates the ways that the maker ethos can be applied to programs and events at your museum or historic site. It will explore how the makerspace can be used outside of the museum, first exploring how it can be used as an outreach tool, and then the ways that the maker ethos can be applied to a variety of offerings your museum or historic site already has, including virtual events and on-site programs.

Key to making effective museum programming that involves historical making is the development of a space for curiosity at your site. Curiosity is what brings people to the makerspace and what makes the makerspace so effective as a learning tool. While what happens in your makerspace can be a wide and diverse array of programmatic offerings, the connecting tissue that binds them is a willingness for the public to engage with the past in a curious way.

PROGRAMMING YOUR HISTORIC MAKERSPACE

As discussed in the previous chapter, much of the regular usage of your makerspace is dependent on the ways your historic site will integrate the makerspace into the site's existing fabric and infrastructure. Your makerspace could be open all the time, or it could be something that only happens at specific events. It could be as large and permanent as a room or as transient as a table or a cart. However, if the makerspace functions on a regular basis, it should be considered as an integral part of the programming that occurs at your site.

Museum programming often falls into a tangled web of mission and revenue. Many organizations see museum programming as a way of generating income for the organization through more visitors going through the door. For some, this is mission-based programming, which focuses on creating events that work to bring the mission of the organization to the public but also generate income. Others have specific programs that generate revenue, and those support mission-based programming.[1] Like any program offering, programming connected to your makerspace will have to interact with this delicate web: it will have to be a part of the broader operations of your organization, which is something to be endlessly aware of. Your makerspace programming will also have to interact with the existing framework of your site. Consider the site, its history, and its people. Plan making around that; making in a historical context has more meaning when it is thematically and programmatically linked to the history of the place where it occurs. Programming connected to your makerspace and the idea of making at your site should be aware of the site and its needs. It should fulfill the organization's needs and the needs of the community. It should help tell the narrative of the site. As stressed in the previous chapter, the work of your makerspace should be tied to the mission, values, and goals of your museum or historical site. This is also the case with programming in your makerspace.

In bringing maker programming to your museum, you should be aware of challenges and hindrances to access, working toward creating programming surrounding the makerspace that focuses on the makerspace as being something for everyone and not just for a small group of people. That focus is one of the themes of this book and should always be considered in maker programming at historic sites. Diverse audiences, perspectives, and ideas are important and should be an intrinsic part of the making of history and making in general. As has been discussed in chapters 1 and 2, the maker movement is not without controversy or places that need to improve, as there are roadblocks of access for individuals who are neither white nor male, as well as for people who have disabilities or different learning abilities. Your programming, like your makerspace, should be constantly aware of this and should work toward creating a space for historical making that is open and available for all.

It's time to put that makerspace to work. One of the most effective ways to do that is to foster curiosity around making at your historic site. It is important, then, that curiosity be explored first.

PROGRAMMING CURIOSITY AT YOUR MAKERSPACE

What does it mean to be curious?

In a March 1952 letter to his biographer Carl Seeling, Albert Einstein stated, humbly, "I have no special talent, I am only passionately curious."[2] While you might not be theorizing about splitting the atom in your historic makerspace, the physicist's admission is an essential mantra that you should use to form the backbone of the culture of your makerspace. When you create an environment for learning new skills, the most important ingredient is not talent or latent skill; it is curiosity. If someone is curious, they will be willing to learn a new skill. At your makerspace, you will provide the rest through programming and experiences: you and your maker team have the tools, the experience, and the knowledge, which you can pass on to your makers. Those makers do not have to have any experience with any of those tools at all; rather, all they need is to have an open mind to experience them. To be a maker is, as Einstein said, to be passionately curious.

One of the most important elements of your makerspace, whatever it might look like, is providing a safe space for curiosity. This is especially important for adult visitors, who might be less willing to engage in learning a new thing because of fears of failure. In order for your makers to have an unfettered sense of curiosity, it is important to create an environment that allows for both success and failure. Modern culture constantly stresses quick, quantitative success. If one does something, they should be able to achieve it with success in a quick and efficient manner. Anyone who makes anything with their hands, from paintings, to chairs, to pies, to clothing, knows that this is not the case when it comes to making, even in the modern world. For any success, there are many failures.[3] For every perfectly made item, there are other items that were frustratedly ripped up, thrown away, or forgotten about. That is the process of making things with one's hands. In order for one to have a meaningful and joyful experience as a maker, especially as an adult, it is important to provide a space where they can have the meaningful and necessary experience of both success and failure: because that is the way humans have been making things for millennia. For the historical makerspace to be effective, one must embrace the realities of making, in that there might not (and probably won't) be immediate success. Once that space is created, curiosity will take over. This can lead to fulfilling maker experiences for your visitors. Below are some ways to create a maker culture that allows both success and failure:

- *Stress the process, not the result.* Making is both about the process and the finished product of that process. While many people might expect to have crafted a perfectly made handmade item, many will be afraid they will not be able to achieve that or will be disappointed when they don't. Some people will have more success than others, especially in the context of a one-time or first-time use of your maker facilities at a program or event. Explain that making is about the process and not necessarily only about the finished product. Craft events that focus on experience rather than tangibility. As we have previously explored (chapters 1 and 2), the Maker Movement is focused on processes and the road to get to a finished product as much as the finished product itself.
- *Celebrate success and support failure.* When someone makes something and is proud of what they have made, it is important to celebrate that success. They did something out of their comfort zone and learned something new. That should be applauded. Likewise, failure is something to be supported and celebrated. There is something to be celebrated in someone's

willingness to try: support and applaud that willingness to try in the same ways you celebrate success. Tell your visitors that the next one they make will be better, and talk to them about the ways in which learning a process itself can tell us much about the past.

- *Create a culture of warmth.* For the above to work, it is important that you create a culture of warmth in your makerspace. This does not mean you need to be constantly applauding or cheering on your visitors. In fact, it's best if you avoid that, especially for adults. It can come across as mocking and disingenuous, which is the opposite of what should be desired. What is key is to create a space that is genuinely and intrinsically warm. Visitor service is important, and creating a space where people feel comfortable asking for help, failing, trying again, and succeeding in equal measures is equally important.
- *Allow for success.* The above considered, it is important to allow for success. This can be as simple as considering the event and audience and choosing a project that will have a less steep learning curve: say candle dipping instead of bobbin lace. Don't be afraid of challenging your makerspace visitors, but be cognizant of your audience and their probable skills and interests. Remember that many casual visitors are visiting your site for something fun to do; try to meet that expectation. The success of people being able to do something—the pure, unadulterated excitement of achieving something that they had previously thought unachievable—could potentially bring them back for more. Then challenge.

THE HISTORICAL MAKERSPACE AND REGULAR PROGRAMMING

Here are a couple possibilities of maker programming that can occur inside the context of your museum or historic site. Of course, the sky's the limit, and programming connected to the makerspace can be as diverse and exciting as the organization and the people who take part in it. I hope, though, that the rest of this chapter provides an idea of the wide list of possibilities that can happen at your site surrounding the idea of making and the makerspace. Further information on the programs described below, in greater detail, can be found in the appendices to this book.

Your historic site probably already has a roster of preexisting programs that occur every year. Those events probably bring with them their own framework, ideas, favorites, and traditions. Many historic sites fall into the trap of thinking that long-standing programming is fine just the way it is, because "we have always done it this way" (someone invariably says). The truth is that long-held programming (even if it is very successful) can sometimes do with a bit of a face-lift. Even if your site has always done something one way, any program can be reinvigorated and given a new perspective. This can make the program meaningful for new visitors, who are experiencing a newly reimagined event. Repeat visitors (the people that come to the same event every year) might have a chance to see the event (and your site) in a new way. Reinvigoration and reimagining a long-held event can be complex and daunting, with a series of stakeholders, volunteers, and elements that need to be brought about. Sometimes changing an event requires a bit of a push. The makerspace at your site can provide just that.

WORKSHOPS

One of the more effective possibilities of programming that can occur connected to your makerspace is the idea of the workshop, which has long been part of the ways in which museums interact with their public. Connected to the makerspace, the workshop can occur in two different ways. It can happen at a prescheduled fixed time or it can happen as part of a series of drop-ins. Here are ways that these can be achieved:

THE "REGULAR" WORKSHOP

The regular workshop is happening at many museums already; maybe you have one! The museum or historic site advertises that a workshop will be done at a specific time and, usually, tickets will be sold ahead of time. At the workshop, participants learn how to do specific crafts or tasks, following the instructions of a facilitator. Usually, they take place over the span of a couple hours. At the end, the visitor leaves having made something.

The workshop fits into the framework of the historic makerspace organically. Workshops present a scheduled opportunity for people to learn a skill or to make something. When infused with the ethos of the makerspace, workshops can become less about the finished product and more about the process. The workshop facilitator should host the workshop in a way that makes sense for your organization and for them. However, in an organization that has embraced the ethos of the makerspace, the workshop provides a space for people to interact with the idea of being a maker. While the maker (and the workshop participant) is interested in the finished product, thinking about the workshop within the language of the makerspace shows that process, not results, is the important part.

The other essential element here is curiosity, the binding glue of the makerspace. In creating workshops where the idea of curiosity is embraced and encouraged, and where people can feel comfortable succeeding or failing, the workshop becomes accessible and meaningful for the public. Likewise, it is a reinforcing of essential skills that are often forgotten in the modern world. While the workshop might be about learning a particular skill, say, for example, basket making, embracing the maker ethos ensures that the workshop is not totally about the basket, whatever the end result might be. Rather, it is about the process of getting to the basket: the time spent making the basket, the time spent learning the techniques necessary to make the basket, and the time spent failing at the techniques necessary for making a basket before succeeding.

THE DROP-IN WORKSHOP

The drop-in workshop can also be very easily applied to the maker ethos. A drop-in workshop is something that many museums (including yours, perhaps) already do. A craft is chosen and the organization sets up a table. A facilitator is stationed at that table during a certain window of time. Participants can stop by and take part in the craft anytime within the window of time that it is available, make the craft, and be on their way. The people that come to drop-in workshops can represent a wide variety of the organization's audience, and can be part of regular attendance to the site or people stopping by just for the workshop, or both. Drop-in workshops are usually most successful as events that are geared toward children and their families.

There are a couple of things to keep in mind when it comes to the drop-in workshop. First, that the process that people will be learning should be quick to explain, easily learned, and quick to do. People participating in a drop-in workshop are not, generally, looking for an all-day event. Instead, they are looking for something quick to do as a family or in addition to the experience that they had at your site.

Second, location is very important when it comes to the drop-in workshop. At one of the sites I worked at, we would have drop-in workshops outside, on the lawn in front of the museum and off of the road. People would stop by and visit us specifically for the drop-in workshop (which, of course, we heavily advertised) while out on their afternoon walk, or on their way to the community pool (which was conveniently located across the street). When planning a series of drop-in workshops, consider how people will be dropping in. If you have a physical makerspace located inside your museum, that might be a place to have the drop-ins. It could be just as effective, though, to use the drop-in as a moment to take the makerspace on the road on your own site (more on taking the makerspace on the road below). Set up a table in a prominent place outside of your museum: meet and make with your community outside of the museum building itself. Another benefit this has is removing the barrier of entry to the museum or historic site. Many can find the imposing building of the museum something that might not be warm or might be a bit off-putting. Seeing someone friendly outside, who is willing to teach them a craft, can remove that barrier of entry to the site itself.

Regularity is incredibly important with drop-in workshops. At that same historic site, we ran drop-in workshops on the first and third Saturdays of the month, during museum operational hours. This worked very well. As a site, we knew exactly when the drop-ins would be and could advertise, staff, and prepare accordingly. Likewise, the community learned that on the first and third Saturdays of the month, drop-in workshops were available. Many families began scheduling their weekends around it.

Both the regular workshop and the drop-in workshop have the possibility of being an entry point for regular use of your makerspace. Attendance at one workshop or drop-in can jolt that all-important spark of curiosity and a visitor can have a sudden passion to learn all sorts of things. As a result, they might start coming to more workshops and might begin utilizing your historic makerspace more often. They might tell a friend, who might tag along, and then that friend might tell their friend, and so on. This chain reaction to getting people into your historic site is not new or a surprise to you, I'm sure. However, when thinking about programming your makerspace and creating a maker culture (as discussed in the previous chapter), the creation of a regular contingent of happy makers is vital.

MAKING ON TAP: THE HISTORY HAPPY HOUR

Sometimes people need to loosen up a bit to let the spark of curiosity hit them. For that, might I suggest bringing the history happy hour to your makerspace? The history happy hour is something that has been part of the current museum world and perhaps your site hosts one already. Normally at a history happy hour there is a fun talk or presentation as well as adult beverages and snacks. History happy hours are a fun night out at the museum, and, while usually advocated as a way to get working millennials into museum doors, can be an exciting evening out for just about everyone of legal drinking age.[4]

The history happy hour can be easily transformed into a makerspace event. For this, it might be helpful to plan backward. Choose a craft that might be of interest for people to learn, and then work backward planning your evening. A history happy hour I once hosted included demonstrations on making Victorian hair mourning jewelry. In part, this happened because of a long-held fascination with hair wreaths and the cultures of mourning that surrounded them that I personally had. And so I, in the spirit of the Maker Movement, set out to learn how to make Victorian mourning jewelry. Paired with a short, informative, and informal talk on mourning traditions, as well as adult refreshments, an event was made. To make the event feel even more special, why not find food that would accompany the sort of historical time period you are going to talk about? For a history happy hour on nineteenth-century mourning, perhaps pair hair wreaths with different kinds of popular nineteenth-century funeral foods and drinks. For a history happy hour about food preservation in the colonial period, why not skew the refreshments to fit the period? A history happy hour can be an experience in its entirety, and provides a place where adults can break free from their regular life, engage creativity in a safe and supportive space, and experience foods and drinks that they might previously not have. If your organization is not equipped to specially create a menu for a happy hour based on the past, choose foods and drinks that are thoughtful and exciting.

CRAFTS AND TRADES WEEKEND

An element of the Maker Movement is the idea of the makeathon or the hackathon. These events are very diverse across the Maker Movement, and can be defined, as Joshua Tauberer has noted in his *How to Run a Successful Hackathon*, as "hacking is creative problem solving (it doesn't have to involve technology). A hackathon is any event of any duration where people come together to solve problems."[5] Tauberer's definition here is broad but helpful. Makeathons or hackathons are often a feature of universities, schools, or libraries and focus on the idea of creating an atmosphere of collaboration over a set time and in a set place, which is often paired with other events, workshops, and judging by a panel of experts.[6] Often, these events are centered around a particular theme or technology, but not always. Likewise, they require that participants complete a large amount of work in a small amount of time.[7] However, these words can prove a stumbling block for people who might not feel that something like a hackathon or a makeathon is a place for them. For this, I am proposing using a more inclusive phrase such as "Crafts and Trades Weekend," which sounds more accessible and less tied to modern buzzwords. A wide variety of terms are possible; name it according to what works at your site.

This event can look like a vast variety of things, depending on the goals of the organization that is hosting it, but at its basics it is an event, held over a short period of time, where a group of makers come together and make things. They solve problems and arrive at outcomes. They might learn new skills. They will get feedback from other makers and from experts. They will be able to interact and form connections with other makers.

The broader concept of a hackathon is very applicable to the idea of the historic makerspace. Already nondependent on modern technology by definition, a historic makeathon could provide a space for people to learn historic trades and crafts together, or to work as part of a community of makers. At a historic makeathon, a theme could be provided (make something out of an animal byproduct, or make something that uses pigments, or make something that uses metal, or something using trades from two different parts of the world), but that is not necessary.

Likewise, the audience for a historic makeathon could be very wide. It could be run with regular people who are regular visitors who are passionate about your museum. You could even wrap it into a "stay at the museum overnight" sort of event, where the making could continue into the night, with pauses for meals and entertainment. Likewise, a historic makeathon could be held with local historic craftsmen or living history interpreters who teach a skill. Many of these historic practitioners in your area most certainly know each other, but they might not have a chance to interact about craft and the things they make away from having to also talk with visitors to whatever event they are at. A makeathon like this can also be a good way to build the community of people who are regularly around your makerspace, to help build the maker culture of your makerspace, and to tap into new veins of knowledge that could be very helpful for the projects you might want to offer as part of your makerspace. Another option for the makeathon could be for your inside stakeholders: your maker team, your volunteers, your board, members of your organization. A sort of insider's makeathon could be an exciting way to bring people in your organization together, to have them problem-solve together, and to help them with building a team around your organization and your makerspace.

While we might think of the past as far from the idea of the hackathon, the idea of the hackathon can be most definitely applied to your historic makerspace.

MAKER PROGRAMMING OUT OF THE MAKERSPACE

But what happens if you want to leave your site and interact with the general public? Or if you want to enjoy the maker ethos without an actual physical space that has been set aside for the makerspace itself?

OUTREACH PROGRAMS

Why not take the makerspace on the road? The makerspace ethos can easily be adapted to move out into the world, as part of other events held by other members of the community.

Most organizations are already tabling at local community days or events. Why not take the makerspace along with you? In this way, you can interact with the community and also interact with people who might be enthusiastic visitors to your in-museum makerspace or your site in general.

Another possibility for outreach is to do a pop-up makerspace. At a pop-up makerspace, your organization creates a temporary makerspace for an agreed-upon amount of time at a certain place, such as setting up your makerspace at your local library, in a local coffee shop, or at a local bookshop. The possibilities are endless. Like a tabling event, this provides an opportunity for your organization and your organization's makerspace to interact with a variety of people from your community it might not otherwise have. It is also a way to form important community partnerships.

The makerspace can also be used for education in schools in your community. Many organizations already have a framework for going into schools and doing an event in the classroom. Why not bring the idea of the historic makerspace there? This could also be applied to the idea of a traveling crate, where teachers can borrow a ready-packed box that has everything they need to do the maker activities (as well as educational resources).

The concerns surrounding these different sorts of outreach programs are similar. Some things to keep in mind are:

- When taking the makerspace on the road, it is even more important to think about your audience and ensure that the project they are doing is accessible, valuable, and does not have a very steep learning curve. While someone who might be attending something like a specific maker event or a history happy hour might be willing to take on a challenge, someone you are encountering in the wild, away from your museum or at an outreach experience in a school, might still want a bit of a challenge but might also want success. Consider the event, its audience, and the people you will likely encounter, and plan accordingly.
- Think of an outreach event a bit like a drop-in workshop. The project should be rewarding and educational, but should also be accessible and scalable. This should be applicable to a variety of things, including materials, budget, and where you are going to be. The project should also be quick: you'll be encountering people who did not necessarily expect to be making something with you. Don't make them spend all day with you.
- It is important to plan in dialogue with your portable makerspace's host. Be sure they know what to expect, and learn their hopes for the event. If you are having an outreach program at the location of a community partner, be sure to stress that partnership and consider the event as a mutually beneficial event.
- Think about the project you are planning on doing and plan ahead. Be sure you have all the right supplies and everything you will need. Likewise, be sure you have materials to clean up, if necessary. It is a good idea to keep everything together, perhaps in a large tote or crate, for ease of moving into and out of the space you will be working in. Talk to whoever is hosting you and be sure that there is a table for you; if not, bring your own. Finally, be sure that any needs you might have (electricity, water, lighting) are available.

As with almost every aspect of the makerspace and historic sites in general, what you do with your makerspace on the road is totally unique to your site, the narrative your site tells, your organization's mission, as well as your community and the needs of the people you will interact with.

THE VIRTUAL MAKERSPACE AND MAKE FROM HOME

This book was written during the COVID-19 pandemic. The pandemic and subsequent shutdowns created a variety of challenges for anyone that interacts with the public. Museums and historic sites are not alone in this. While many sites had to deal with the harsh reality of being closed, without visitorship and revenue, for the majority of 2020, many of those same sites found new and innovative ways to interact with the public. Zoom lectures, take-home crafts, and outdoor events became popular and essential. It is important to consider the makerspace as something that can be adapted to the necessity for online interaction or something that could have an online component outside of a pandemic.

Part of what makes a historic makerspace important is the physicality of the makerspace and the tangible reality of learning how to make something by hand. I believe that historical making is important because it pushes individuals to make something by hand. This experience is incredibly difficult to adapt to a virtual environment, but it is not impossible. Here are some possibilities:

- *Take-home maker kits.* Take-home maker kits are a way for your makers to bring the makerspace into their own home. They should include all of the materials needed for a project, as well as instructions. It might be particularly helpful to make instructions that are both textual and visual, for different sorts of learners. A solution might be to create a YouTube video showing a particular skill being done and then including the URL or a QR code that could bring the maker to that video. Likewise, you could have an agreed-upon Makerhour, where guests can join an on-site maker on Zoom or another video-conferencing program, and could ask questions of someone live.
- *Videos and how-tos.* The internet is filled with videos and how-tos, showing people how to do anything from installing electrical fixtures to changing the oil in a car. Why not create videos that show how a historical process works as part of your makerspace? These could be hosted on YouTube or on your website. If you get particularly adventurous, they could even become part of your historic site's social media presence. They can provide useful information, show your site as a credible source for that information, and advertise the great things that are going on at your site.
- *Online instructions.* This is a less interactive version, but your website could include instructions on how to do historic crafts that someone might be able to learn in your makerspace. These instructions should be crafted for a wide variety of users and learners.

These are just a sampling of the possibilities of ways that your makerspace can become virtual. Through the COVID-19 pandemic, the shift to the virtual was essential. However, the skills learned during the pandemic should continue to be used in the post-pandemic world. Virtual programming in your makerspace can help reach new audiences—audiences who might not even be within the same geographical area as your historic site. In a world that is becoming increasingly more digital, that is very important. However, it is equally important to not forget the things that are in the DNA of the historic makerspace: tangible experience and the importance of learning to make with one's hands. In crafting virtual experiences, always keep the tangible in mind.

MAKERSPACE PROGRAMMING WITHOUT A MAKERSPACE

Your organization does not have to have a designated makerspace in order to take part in makerspace programming. In fact, the vast majority of the programs mentioned in this chapter could be easily scaled into any organization even if it didn't have a physical makerspace. It does not require a makerspace to have drop-in workshops, making events, outreach programs, or history happy hours. In fact, the maker ethos can be applied to any sort of organization as needed.

NOTES

1. Margaret W. Hughes, "Bridging the Divide: Mission and Revenue in Museum Programming," *Journal of Museum Education* 35, no. 3 (2010): 279–88. Hughes presents a series of case studies of organizations that juggle this difficult balance.
2. Albert Einstein, "Letter to Carl Seeling, March 11, 1952," Einstein Archives (Hebrew University of Jerusalem, Jerusalem).
3. Failure is an important tool for education. This has been particularly well articulated by Dennis L. Weisman in his "An Essay on the Art and Science of Teaching," in which Weisman explores the thoughts of inventor Charles Franklin Kettering and how they apply to education. Weisman notes that learning from failure, or "Intelligent failure," is an important tool for gaining new skills and knowledge. Dennis L. Weisman, "An Essay on the Art and Science of Teaching," *American Economist* 57, no. 1 (2012): 111–25.
4. Aleah Vinick and Rachel Abbot, "How to Design Programs for Millennials," *History News* 70, no. 4 (2015): 1–8.
5. Joshua Tauberer, "How to Run a Successful Hackathon," https://hackathon.guide.
6. As Tauberer notes, "training workshops is a great way to give them something to do that they will be more comfortable with than diving into hacking. You can run workshops to introduce participants to the subject of the hackathon or to particular technical skills useful for the hackathon. Workshops can also be places to have a discussion about issues in the field related to the hackathon. Workshops should be interactive as much as possible." Ibid.
7. Andrew Jason Turner, Caroline D. Hardin, and Matthew Berland, "Hackathons and 'I'dentities: Museum Visitor Identities in Other Informal Learning Environments," *Visitor Studies* 24, no. 1 (2021): 184.

6

Re-creating the Past

In the novel *The Go-Between*, author L. P. Hartley famously muses that "the past is a different country, they do things differently there."[1] Hartley had a point: the world of the past was very different from our own, though it can tell us a lot about the present. Hartley's musing can also be applied to learning a historic trade or craft. While trades or crafts can be similar to what we do today, they can also be very different and can result in unexpected problems and challenges. Learning them can require thinking about the past in very different ways.

This chapter is a road map for exploring the different country of the past through hands-on making. In it, we are going to explore a methodology for re-creating historic processes and address some of the problems that can arise in bringing a historic process to life today.

RE-CREATING THE PAST: A METHODOLOGY

Learning a historic process is difficult for anyone. Many people who are historic makers talk about the length of time that it takes to master a trade or craft, as well as the support systems they need along the way. You will not become an expert in a historic trade overnight; in fact, you probably won't become an expert in a year. Many people have the resources and support network for learning a historic trade. It is important to contact those resources; nothing is better than learning firsthand from someone.

This chapter discusses, in part, learning a historic trade that is connected to your site, area, or interests when there might not be someone readily available to teach it to you. Do not see that as a stumbling block; rather, embrace the industrious spirit of the Maker Movement and learn it yourself!

This section proposes a methodology for re-creating processes from the past from scratch that I have found to be particularly helpful. In my view, this method allows for the right ratio of research, experimentation, practice, and troubleshooting to produce meaningful results.

WHAT IS A METHODOLOGY AND WHY HAVE ONE?

A methodology is a framework that is applied to any sort of research or practice. It provides a road map for approaching a problem. In academic practices, a methodology is used as a way to approach and to frame research. Within the field of history, a historian can apply all sorts of methodologies to study the past. For example, someone interested in ethnohistory will be interested in the ways in which anthropological theory can help understand human cultures of the past. A social historian might study the past by looking at the things that people had and quantifying them or by studying census data. Methodologies are important frameworks for making research more meaningful and fruitful.

What does methodology have to do with learning a historical trade? A lot, actually. While much of learning a new craft or skill comes down to playing around and trial and error, re-creating a historic trade or craft should be done thoughtfully and deliberately. When you are re-creating a historic process, you are doing more than having fun with an art project; you are creating a tool for the engagement with the past, opening the door for both makers in your site's makerspace and yourself to interact with the past in a new and meaningful way. This is not something that should be attempted lightly or without research. Just as researching to create an exhibit or researching to work on a new interpretation of your site is a vital way for telling dynamic and impactful stories about the past, so, too, is researching a historic trade.

The methodology proposed in this chapter is not necessarily tied to a historical approach. It will not be advocating for the use of a particular framework to study the past. However, it provides a framework that could be helpful as you go through the process. Any historical process will look very different. The resources that will be available for your use and research will be different. Below is a six-step process for re-creating a historic trade. Your personal experiences will vary, but the steps below provide a road map for the process that involves thoughtful planning, research, experimentation, and reflection.

STEP ONE: ASK QUESTIONS

Asking questions is a good first step to make when one is beginning to learn a historic trade. It is important to get situated with yourself, what you want to learn, and why. Here are some questions to consider before delving into research:

- *Why do I want to learn this trade?* The why of whatever trade you are choosing to learn can be very different: maybe it's something that has long been connected to your historic site or region, or maybe it's just something that has always interested you and you always wanted to learn. Do you want to learn this trade for use in your site's makerspace? Is it something that you want to be able to teach the public? Are you wanting to learn it as a tool for your own research or for research associated with the site? To help preserve it (see chapter 7)?

- *What will this trade contribute to my makerspace? To my site?* Of course, you can use this book and the processes in it outside of a historic site or a makerspace at a historic site, but one of the main suppositions here is that what you do will be part of a historic makerspace. Just like in chapter 4 when the makerspace was crafted to be part of the mission and vision of your historic site, so, too, should the projects and practices that get highlighted there. Maybe the historic trade in question has long been part of your site's history, is part of your site's collection, is part of local history, or is part of your site's period of interpretation. Maybe it will be a trade that fills a hole in your makerspace programming (for example, adding a craft that is not textile based to a very textile-heavy makerspace). There are many reasons to choose a particular craft to learn and to bring into the makerspace, but it is important to consider what your makerspace, the people who make it, and your site in general will gain from it.
- *What are some of the challenges inherent in this trade? For myself? For my site? For my site's visitors?* Any historic trade brings with it challenges, both seen and unforeseen. At any step in the research and reconstruction process, the question of the challenge of the trade should be forefront in your mind. What challenges are a part of this trade that would need to be overcome to learn it? What challenges might make this trade difficult to teach to museum visitors who are using the makerspace? What challenges might this trade pose to the site? Some trades might simply be too difficult to be part of a regular rotation for something like a drop-in workshop, but might be something that could apply to skilled makers or specific workshops. Keep your audience of makers and your museum visitors in mind. Likewise, some trades might be too dangerous to be a part of a regular rotation in your makerspace or for your audience; keep that in mind.

Of course, as always, there are many other questions that might be applicable for you and for your site. As you continue on to further steps, more questions might come to the forefront or might be answered. It is a good idea to keep a record of these as you go; it is good to refer back to and to keep in mind.

STEP TWO: RESEARCH

Hopefully, having done step one, you have identified why you want to learn a particular craft, what it will bring to your makerspace, and some of the challenges that might be a part of bringing that trade to life. No matter what you think you know about a historic process, there is always more to know and things that will surprise you. That is why research is so intrinsically important for learning about the past. There are a wide variety of steps you can take here, and the particular methods that you use might be different depending on what you are researching, but your research should consist of the following:

- *Archival research.* The one necessary component of historical research is a trip to the archives to access primary documents (firsthand accounts and historic texts). Luckily, in the modern world of the internet, a trip to the archives can be very simple. There is much to be learned about a historic trade through a trip to the archives. Many historic trades (especially in the nineteenth century) had books and guides that were aimed toward talking about the knowledge of those trades. Sometimes, certain trades will have historically produced how-to manuals (those are very exciting; they can also present their own challenges). These sorts of guides and texts can be readily available online through university libraries, open-access archives, and sometimes even public libraries.

- *Secondary source research.* When learning a historic trade, it is helpful to know more about that trade and how it functioned. While secondary sources (sources written by scholars) might not tell how to do a historic trade or craft, they will help contextualize the trade within its world. This is important for the "why?": Why is this an important trade to learn? What does it bring to your museum's programming and to your historic maker-space as a whole?

- *Material culture.* If you are reading this book, there is a good chance that you are connected to a historic site in one way or another. One of the things that helps define historic sites is their collections. An important step in the research process of learning a historic trade is to look at historic examples of that trade. Some of them might be in your site's own collection! Interested in learning how to make a hair wreath (as I did below)? Have a look at one of the examples in your collection! Interested in learning how to dye cloth? Have a look at historic textiles in your collection! This is not just looking at the object ("oh, how cool!"); rather, it is studying the object. Get close and look at the ways it is put together (without damaging or hurting the integrity of the object, of course). Use a magnifying glass, take photos, make drawings and diagrams, and take notes. While an archival how-to manual might be very helpful in learning your historic trade, there is no better document for how to make something than the thing itself. Ideally, it is a good idea to reference the tangible historic object as you go through the process of learning the trade. Perhaps even try to replicate it!

- *Material research.* A final mode of research that you should embark on is informed by both archival research and looking at an object itself: researching the materials. What materials does your archival research indicate you need to use for the project? Where would those materials have been acquired historically? How would they have been used historically? Where can you acquire them now? This leads into step three.

STEP THREE: MATERIALS

This step can be simultaneously the easiest and the hardest step. Simply acquire the materials you need to learn the process. For some historic processes, this could be easy: maybe you just need some yarn or something else readily available. Other historic processes will be harder: maybe you'll need something more complicated, like specialized equipment, tools, or materials that aren't readily available. What this step looks like depends a lot on what you are attempting to learn.

In many ways, the past was a different country. One of the ways that this is most apparent is safety. In the preindustrial world, there was little consideration for safety in the workplace. Likewise, many people worked trades that exposed them to dangerous chemicals and materials on a daily basis. As historians, we should not necessarily think that "they didn't know better"; rather it was the reality of their lives, which was different from our own. However, we should be fully aware of the materials that we are using, as well as the ways in which they can impact our health, the health of our visitors, and the health of the environment.

Some materials that were used in the past were very dangerous, including corrosive chemicals and materials like arsenic and lead. Of course, these should be avoided. Some historic processes might be difficult to do without avoiding dangerous materials. In the context of the makerspace at your historic site, they might be best ignored. Likewise, some materials might not be accessible or might not be ethical, and will need to be swapped for other materials. This, as with everything, depends on the process you are trying to learn. Here are some thoughts to help:

- *Safety concerns.* Some materials and processes for historic making might be dangerous, and should not be used by an untrained general public (or, sometimes, by any people at all). This can include dangerous materials such as arsenic and lead. Some safety concerns can be answered by the audience for this trade at your site: Is this something you are willing to teach just yourself as a research tool or do you want to teach it to others? Safety measures should be followed in either case, but some things might be less a concern if just something that you personally would like to learn. Unless the process is dependent on particular materials, adaptation for a safer material that will do the same thing is always a good idea.
- *Unavailable materials.* Some materials might be unavailable in the modern world. Unavailable materials can include raw materials as well as specialized tools for trades that have become more mechanized or have fallen out of favor. For example, it can be exceptionally hard to find the specific sorts of cutting knives for shoemaking that would have been used in the eighteenth and nineteenth centuries. Sometimes materials and tools can be substituted for these unavailable things. Other times, the process might

be dependent on them. A good course of action here can be to contact people who are working with the historic trade you want to learn; they might have some ideas for sourcing or replacing materials.

- *Unethical or illegal materials.* Some materials are unethical or illegal for use. Particularly, one could think of ivory, which was once a very popular material but is now (rightfully) a protected material. While laws might not have existed in the past surrounding the use of a material, it is vitally important that you follow laws surrounding protected materials in the present day.
- *Environmental consciousness.* The Industrial Revolution in particular was a vital turning point toward the pollution of the planet. Many historic skills from before, during, and after the Industrial Revolution brought with them hazardous effects on the environment. It is always vitally important, regardless of what your research finds, that you dispose of and use materials in such a way as to be environmentally conscious.

While materials can sometimes be the easy part, as this step shows they can also be very complicated. Before getting to work and making a thing, it is very important that you both are using the correct tools for replicating the historical process in question and that you are using materials and tools that are safe for yourself, eventual future makers at your site, and the planet.

STEP FOUR: TRY IT OUT

Now you have your research and the materials, so try the thing! Make a thing! Odds are, your first attempt at your chosen historic trade will be less than stellar and you will not want to show it to anyone. That's okay. In the previous chapter, this book stressed the importance of creating a safe space for the exploration of creativity, and a place where both failure and success were part of the learning experience. In that context, it was about creating a space for makers in your historic makerspace to try, fail, learn, and succeed. However, it is important to apply that same feeling and attitude toward your own work in learning a trade that you will eventually teach to people. You will fail, at least at first. Accept that as part of the learning process and learn from it. Most importantly, don't just take the thing you have made and failed at and throw it promptly in the trash. Do an autopsy on it. What went wrong and why? How could the outcome be changed? What would be different if you did something in a different way? Just as you counted the idea of archival and material research as part of the process of learning, so, too, count the process of actually making; that is part of the research itself (which will be explored more in the next chapter). Take notes, record your findings, and learn from them.

STEP FIVE: GO BACK TO THE DRAWING BOARD

Step five is all important but is often forgotten. By the time you have reached step five, you will have chosen a historic trade to learn; you will have questioned why you want to learn that and what will be gained from it; you will have researched the trade, its materials, and its processes; and you will have done it (and probably, at least at first, failed at it). Going back to the drawing board, so to speak, is pivotal here. Is what you learned as you did the process what you expected? Did it support the historical research that you did? Do you feel that you missed something? Just as you began the process by asking questions, so, too, should you enter the end game of the process with questions.

STEP SIX: PRACTICE THE PRACTICE

Practice makes perfect. That is a cliche at this point, but it is also true. Remember that people in the past (the people who made the material culture object you were learning from, in fact) made it, probably, after years of learning, apprenticing, and honing their craft. Do not expect to be an expert overnight, or, in fact, an expert over a short period of time. The amount of practice you put in here might vary depending on your needs and the needs of the site: maybe you want to learn a bunch of historic trades so you and your site have a wide arsenal available for your use in your makerspace. Less practice might be okay then. Or, maybe, you want to become your site's expert on one particular thing: then more practice would be warranted. There is no correct answer here. It is important to note, though, that if you plan on teaching the process to visitors or users of your makerspace, you should be pretty adept at the process and all that can (and will) go wrong. Likewise, keep in mind that you will gain new insights into the process as you teach it (and as you teach it over and over, and as you see people learn it). There is no prescriptive reality for the amount of time that you need to put into learning a craft before you can teach it to others. It is important, though, that you have developed a familiarity with the process, can replicate it, and can do so in a way that is as faithful to the past as possible.

The thing about making and practicing the art of making is that it can be both rewarding and frustrating; it also, as this book posits, places the historian in tangible contact with the processes of the past.

A HAIRY EXAMPLE

It might be hard to imagine how this process could work when faced with the abstract. I would now like to provide an example from my own work of what this methodology for learning a historic trade can be, with the strange and interesting historic craft of hair work.

THE HAIR WORK: A MEDITATION AND A CASE STUDY

Hair work is part of a series of traditions connected to mourning. Mourning, of course, is ancient and has been going on since people have died. When modern people think of mourning, we often think of the complex traditions of wearing black, covering mirrors, reorganizing one's social calendar, and more. These traditions were tied to a specific time and place: in the United States and

Great Britain in the mid-nineteenth century. In England, this time was marked by the death of Prince Albert, Queen Victoria's husband, in 1861, and her subsequent public mourning. In the United States, this period of time was during the American Civil War.

Hair was given as a memento since antiquity, and would often be kept in jewelry or in a locket. In the mid-nineteenth century, the art of hair work entered the mourning world. Mourners would collect the hair of loved ones, and weave it with wires to create flowers and other shapes. Professional hair workers advertised their services in newspapers and in the Sears catalog, but many chose to do their own hair work themselves. Patterns were published in books and as part of housekeeping magazines. Hair is a part of the body that does not decay, and making it into an art piece was a way for people to have a tangible reminder of the person they had lost, to hold their very essence in their hands and to keep it as a personal memento for years to come.

Enter, then, me and hair art. In my experience, when people encounter this artform they usually have one of two reactions: horror and revulsion or deep fascination. I've always been the second. It was always high on my list of historic crafts to learn. When I set out to learn to make hair art (or hair work, as many of the nineteenth-century sources call it), I had no experience doing it at all. I began by asking why it was something I wanted to learn: I thought it would be a fun challenge and I also expected to use it at my historic site's October History Happy Hour (which I did). Then I set out to research. In researching, I consulted three sources. First, I consulted secondary sources on hair work and the role of hair art within systems of mourning.[2] Armed with that background knowledge, I felt relatively confident to then delve into the primary documentation. Luckily for me (and for people wanting to learn hair work!), there are how-to manuals that exist! Two that I found particularly helpful for my work were Mark Campbell, *Self Instructor in the Art of Hair Work, Dressing Hair, Making Curls, and Hair Jewelry of Every Description* (1867), and William Halford and Charles Young, *The Jewellers' Book of Patterns in Hair Work: Containing a Great Variety of Copper-Plate Engravings of Devices and Patterns in Hair: Suitable for Mourning Jewelry, Brooches, Rings, Guards, Alberts, Necklets, Lockets, Bracelets, Miniatures, Studs, Earrings, etc., etc., etc.* (1864; no one made titles like authors in the nineteenth century). At the time of my research, both of these incredibly helpful texts were available online.[3] The final source I accessed was hair wreaths themselves, both in person and through digital collections online. I wish I could say that the above research—secondary, primary, and the object itself—made me feel somewhat confident to make some hair work. In some ways, it made me more confused: there is nothing more opaque sometimes than a vaguely illustrated nineteenth-century instructional text. At some point, though, I felt as ready as I ever would be to go on to the next step and try to make some hair work.

Having done the research, I knew there were different versions of hair work that could be created. I settled on one of the simpler ones, which I knew would be easier to try and easier to teach. I also knew that it involved only a small amount of materials: wire, a piece of wood to wrap around, an optional clamp, gum arabic, and, of course, hair (ideally around a foot in length, and ideally a nicely sized lock of hair). The first four things I had at my disposal already, but the hair I questioned. I had no problem using hair to make hair work with (why not?), but I had a hunch that using actual human hair (and, probably, human hair from a stranger) could present a possible problematic barrier for people who might be wanting to learn how to make hair work. Hair is something that often brings with it a very visceral reaction. I settled on doll hair, and purchased a bag at a local craft store. I was dubious it would act like actual hair, but thought it was worth giving it a try.

Then I did the thing. With many mumbled bad words, I managed to make a somewhat feebly made piece of hair work. The process is both complex and simple, and relies on the regular weaving of hair around a dowel, which is then held into place with two wires. The process, then, involves repetition. I stared at it, and then began to do a bit of an autopsy on it: What worked and what didn't? What could be done better next time? Was I wrapping too tight or too loose? More importantly, was this a pretty honest representation of the craft as a whole: Did I do it right? Having answered those questions, somewhat, I tried it a couple more times, and felt more confident. At least confident enough to try to teach it to other people. As it turns out, the doll hair did work.

It would be a lie to say that the first time teaching hair work to makers at my historic site went without a hitch. It has a very steep learning curve and requires the right combination of skill and confidence. I attempted to create that safe space for exploration and failure, which actually ended up working. There were successes ("Look! I can't believe I did it!"), failures ("I'm just going to hang out here and have my drink instead"), and somewhere in betweens ("Maybe I'll just braid it?"). In creating that positive space, though, the mood was light and a group of adults who had never even considered making hair art before were having a go at it.

My little case study here shows the methodology mentioned above through a real-world lens, and, I hope, shows the ways in which the learning and eventual teaching of a historic trade can work and some of the problems and challenges that can come as a result. Through the application of a coherent approach and methodology, those problems can become identified and solved. Some things to take away from my experience:

- *Process over product.* As has been mentioned in previous chapters, remember to focus on the process rather than the end product, especially as you are beginning to learn a historic trade through this process of research and reconstruction. The first thing you make will look horrible (my first attempt at hair work was). The second might still be horrible, but eventually you will have something that looks somewhat presentable. The important part is the honing of the process and the skill: you are using different mental and physical muscles than you have before, and learning an entirely new skill.

- *Rinse and repeat.* Repetition is key, as is step five of the methodology. It doesn't matter if you are able to sort of do something once. Instead, you have to do that several times. The first thing you make learning something new will be a mess (I've said this, but I can't stress it enough). They will get increasingly better. Remember when you did research of the process you wanted to learn through primary and secondary sources? You were gaining an intellectual knowledge of the process that allowed you to learn how to do it. Doing the process itself is also a way to gain knowledge, and continuing to do that process over and over is a way to gain increased knowledge of that.
- *Informed, but keep it light.* Arm yourself with research of the process and with the knowledge you have gained from doing the process, but go into the process with enthusiasm and joy at making something. This is especially important when you are teaching the process to someone, too: remember how long it took you to master the process and treat them with the same kindness you would have liked to have been treated with as you were learning.
- Adhere to safety procedures in place for your site and your makerspace. Be safe, but remember that nothing you are doing is brain surgery; your craft will not die on the table if you mess up.

An important thing to remember, too, is that you are not alone. There are people that can help you learn historic trades and crafts; some of them are part of the history community and some of them are right in your site's backyard.

FRIENDS IN HISTORIC PLACES

While part of my hope with this chapter is to empower you to learn and attempt to master a historic trade yourself, it is also important to know that there are friends who can help you. While researching and attempting to learn a historic trade on your own might be fun and rewarding, knowledge of how to do many historic trades continues into the present day in reenactment communities, among historians, on historic sites, and among a variety of professional organizations.

Some people who might be able to help you learn a historic trade have already been identified: they are the people who are connected to your historic site, are stakeholders of your site, and might be part of your makerspace team already. Some others might not have been. Here are some possible people and organizations which might be helpful:

- *Reenactors and living historians.* Reenactors and living historians are regular partners with historic sites, and your site might already have a slate of local reenactors. They might also be part of your makerspace already. Reenactors and living historians are invaluable resources for the history community: tap into them!
- *Historians.* Many historians and scholars of material culture like art historians conduct research on historic trades and processes.
- *Tradespeople.* Tradespeople are skilled makers already, and they might be a helpful resource for learning specific trades or crafts.
- *Artists and artisans.* Artists and artisans are trained makers already, and many of them might be using materials, techniques, and processes that could be part of a historic trade or craft or might be a historic trade as it is.
- *Professional networks.* Depending on where you are, there are all sorts of professional networks that might be helpful for the learning of a historic trade or craft. People who make things, especially people who make things that are very unique, often tend to flock together. A professional organization that might be particularly helpful for learning a historic trade is the Association of Living History, Farm, and Agricultural Museums (ALHFAM), which has listservs, groups, and resources available for members.[4]

The people who are available locally might change depending on the local community and community resources. However, a wide variety of people is always available to talk through an online meeting.

In this chapter, you were equipped to learn a historic trade or craft, researched it, and re-created it from the bottom up using resources and your own research. You also explored some of the ways that learning a historic trade or craft can pose challenges that need to be overcome. The thread that connected it all, though, was the importance of conducting historical research to re-create a historic trade or craft in a way that is historically responsible. In the next chapter, that research will be used to conduct new research. While making is a valuable tool for engaging your museum's audience with the past, it is also a powerful research tool.

NOTES

1. L. P. Hartley, *The Go-Between* (New York: New York Review Books, 1953), 17.
2. Some examples of secondary sources I consulted are Mütter Museum, *A Brief History of Hair Art as Seen in Woven Strands: The Art of Human Hair Work* (Philadelphia: Mütter Museum, 2018); Helen Sheumaker, *Love Entwined: The Curious History of Hairwork* (Philadelphia: University of Pennsylvania Press, 2007).
3. Mark Campbell, *Self-Instructor in the Art of Hair Work, Dressing Hair, Making Curls, Switches, Braids, and Hair Jewelry of Every Description* (New York: Campbell, 1867); William Halford and Charles Young, *The Jewellers' Book of Patterns in Hair Work: Containing a Great Variety of Copper-Plate Engravings of Devices and Patterns in Hair: Suitable for Mourning Jewelry, Brooches, Rings, Guards, Alberts, Necklets, Lockets,*

Bracelets, Miniatures, Studs, Earrings, etc., etc., etc. (William Halford and Charles Young: London, 1864).

4. The Association of Living History, Farm, and Agricultural Museums, www.alhfam .org.

7

Making as History

This chapter is a call to action. As has been explored in the previous chapters, historical making is far more than a gimmick for programming at a historic site. It is a dynamic way for historic sites to tell their story and to engage visitors, both new and old. However, historic making can be far more than that. This chapter explores the ways that learning and teaching a historic craft can help with researching the past and can shed new light on historic trades, historic tradespeople, and the things they made. Learning and teaching a historic craft can also help keep a craft alive.

RESEARCHING A TANGIBLE PAST

History as a discipline is built through using documentary sources to tell a version of the past. Through reading texts (and sometimes between the lines of a text), a historian makes inferences and interpretations of the past. Texts can tell us much. But the world we live in is far more than what exists on paper, and it takes more than paper to unlock the past. Imagine for a moment that someone attempted to reconstruct your life, your job, and the things you do using only paper materials you created, the census, and tax documentation. They would certainly be able to find out a lot about you. However, you could also argue there would be a lot that would be missed: they might not know how you take your coffee, how you do your job, how you like to tend your garden. Much of what we do is lost to history (even in this current era of social media and the digital age, which both exists forever and is lost in an instant). Much of the past is lost to history. This is not to say that using methodologies to unlock the past will peel back the curtain and will leave everyday life of people in the past visible and seeable. The way history is written (academically, for a wider audience, and at historic sites) favors the written word above everything else. It is the most valuable source for describing the past, and from historical texts much can be gleaned about the past and the people who lived within it. This is not always the case for history itself: in fact, it can leave many holes in historical knowledge.

A good, existing, methodological framework to consider the power of making can be found with experimental archaeology. This subfield of the broader field of archaeology is a method of researching where archaeologists can learn about the past through the replication of processes from the past, which is often done to test a hypothesis.[1] As Frederick W. F. Foulds has noted, experimental archaeology can be helpful in that it can succeed in "not only providing the means to 'get inside the minds' of past populations, but also the ability to test the processes of data acquisition, as well as the conclusions and hypotheses that are formulated from such data. At its core, experimental archeology enables us to interpret the material record in a realistic manner."[2] Programs such as Kent State University's Experimental Archaeology Laboratory study ancient technologies such as metalworking, shaping flint tools, and ceramics by studying existing examples, reverse engineering them, and testing them out through experimentation.[3] Experimental archaeology, like archaeology itself, is a scientific process. It asks a hypothesis and then works toward proving that hypothesis through experimentation. If experimentation seems to prove (or disprove) the hypothesis, the experiment is continued to see replicable results. These are the main tenets of science: results in experimentation should be replicable and, thereby, somewhat provable. One-offs are more outliers than indicators of the results of the experiment.

In our makerspaces and as historians in general, we often avoid the idea of the scientific method. Likewise, this book is not calling for a scientific approach to the study of historic processes. Rather, it is calling for an understanding of the power of making as a tool for getting into the shoes (and gloves) of a person from the past, from learning the processes they learned and using that information to gain deeper insight into the past, the people who lived in it, and about objects in our museums' collections. The modern world has created boxes between disciplines: history is part of the humanities and science is part of the sciences. If the Maker Movement teaches us anything, it is that there is a very blurry line between disciplines: they cannot be cordoned off from each other and exist in constant dialogue with each other. A maker in a historic makerspace has to have a wide array of knowledge that centers around their craft as well as the ways the materials of their craft work. To make, then, is to engage in science. Experimental archaeology is an important and powerful tool and places modern-day humans within a scientific framework for understanding the past, giving scholars the tools to decode the processes of the past in a responsible, scientifically truthful way. This can be very informative for the use of experimental archaeology-like frameworks as a historical tool. Making can be a valuable tool for uncovering the past for historians in museums and for historians in academia; in fact, given the particularly valuable role that making can have in museums, it can be used as a tool for bridging the divide between public and academic history, between the history that people write about and the history that people can experience in a tactile way—the history that was lived.

Rather than just reading about a craftsman or a particular tool, learning to do a process can uncover a wide variety of questions that a historian sitting and just looking at a piece of paper might take for granted. It can raise new questions that they might not have considered. The holes in historical knowledge become very painfully evident when one attempts to reconstruct a historical process.

Here are two examples of how this could work in the wild:

- To return to my previous example of hair work and mourning jewelry, learning the process of making hair art helped illuminate a particularly intriguing object that is in many museum collections: the hair wreath. Experiencing the tactility of holding hair in the hands, of moving that hair around, of being in contact with it, can help illuminate that hair art was more about the process—of holding, of making, of being in contact with a material from the body of a loved one, of having a space for mourning, rather than the finished product, as much of an heirloom as that finished object might be. Learning to make hair art also made the object of the hair wreath come alive, and the object could be better talked about and understood. Likewise, teaching the process to visitors can help them gain insight into the object itself, seeing it as a dynamic, living object rather than as a static strange curiosity.
- Learning to cook on a hearth is a totally different experience than learning to cook on a modern stove. Many different skill sets and concerns present themselves. Likewise, many historic recipes (or receipts) are written very differently from modern ones, with vague measurements or instructions. Often, they acted as a sort of mental placeholder for the greater process. Learning to cook a historic recipe is about trial and error, and often by learning through the experience of deciphering the recipe and trying many different versions based on knowledge of the period the recipe comes from. Historic foodways come to life by cooking them. By learning a recipe, and through the trial and error of learning that recipe, a historian can gain a broader understanding of the ways in which recipes functioned, the availability and use of technologies and ingredients, and the scope of work in the kitchen.

These are just two examples, but both show the ways the actual use of materials can help illuminate scholarship and lead to a broader understanding of a historical time period. This can be applied to a wide variety of historical questions. Both of these examples rely on experimental archaeological methodologies to ask a question of the past. Both involve scholars using and learning the processes and materials of the past to answer a historical question, and both show the power of making, and, in some ways, the power of personal experience.

Personal experience is the problem when it comes to scholarship. For traditional academia, personal experience does not matter; the sources do. In the case of history, that is important, since it allows the past to speak for itself through the trained and skilled eye of the historian. In using a carefully thought-out methodology, the problem of personal experience becomes less of a problem. By laying out the parameters, by fully researching the process, and by repeating the process, variables can be eliminated and the process of making—something very fluid and changing—can be used to ask important historical questions.

What then of the museum? The makerspace you have created at your historic site is a powerful tool. It is a powerful tool for community engagement and for the formation of community. Likewise, it is a powerful tool that can be deployed for the forging of new historical knowledge. Here are some ways how:

- Research is part of the work that a museum does. In the endless cycle of programming, school tours, events, and fundraising, it is easy (especially at smaller sites) to lose the integral reality that historic sites are places where research happens: through exhibits, new interpretation, talks, and workshops, we research the past and present it to the public. Making can be a part of this. At my site, the Morgan Log House in Lansdale, Pennsylvania, our site has a history of cloth making in the eighteenth century. To help bring this to life for the public, we have done extensive research on the processes which would have been employed by cloth makers in the eighteenth century in southeastern Pennsylvania, and then worked to replicate them. This helps make the past more dynamic for us (we can answer questions about it easier), and it also helps bring the past to life for our visitors (just how does a spinning wheel work, anyway?).
- Your museum or historic site is a place where research happens, too. Why not use your makerspace to re-create objects in your collection in faithful ways. This can answer all sorts of questions about the ways in which those objects were made (and can cause new questions to be asked!). Likewise, in the end, you can create a reproduction artifact that can be used as part of your organization's educational collection.
- The odds are very high that your museum or historic site is located near a college or university. That college will have professors, but it might also have graduate students who are working on master's theses and dissertations, which could relate to the material culture collections that are part of your museum. Academic departments can be a good source of skilled intellectual labor for museums. It could be a good idea to reach out to the chair of your local history or art history department and explain your makerspace, and work to create a project where students or a scholar can work on a maker project as a tool for their own research.

- Make the fact that your historic site is a place where historic making occurs part of your organizational mission; reach out to academics who work on questions that could be answered by your makerspace or to the broader historical community at large. Your makerspace is a place where experts and amateurs come together and engage their crafts; it can also be a place where new ideas of history can be forged, for your visitors and for historians.

Research can happen in the makerspace. While it is an important tool for engaging the community and for bringing your historic site to life in dynamic ways, it can also be an important tool for asking new questions of the past, both inside and outside of your museum.

Here we have seen the important ways that making can help illuminate the artifacts in museum collections and can bring them to life as an educational tool and not as a static, precious object. In the next section, we will explore what happens when we consider historic processes themselves as another artifact in our collection and in our care.

PROCESS AS ARTIFACT: INTERROGATING AND PRESERVING INTANGIBLE CULTURAL HERITAGE

The processes of the past are an important artifact that museums and historic sites, as well as historians and historical makers, should work toward preserving. They are an invaluable intangible cultural heritage, and once they are gone, they are very difficult to bring back. As makers with historic makerspaces, it is important to be very aware of what the processes of the past mean in the broader arc of history and culture.

Intangible cultural heritage is traditions, conceptualizations, and processes that are an important part of culture and are passed down from person to person. Intangible cultural heritage can include oral traditions, performances and performing arts, social practices, rituals, festival events, knowledge and practices that center around understanding the world and the universe, and, most importantly for this project, knowledge and skills needed to produce traditional crafts.[4] The United Nations Educational, Scientific, and Cultural Organization (UNESCO) notes that intangible cultural heritage is not something that exists solely in the past; it is something that is both traditional and contemporary at the same time: a dynamic process over time. Intangible cultural knowledge is inclusive: it "contributes to social cohesion, encouraging a new sense of identity and responsibility."[5] Intangible cultural heritage is representative: it thrives on its communicability, of its being passed from one generation to the next, of its being transmitted to the community or to other communities. Finally, it is community based, meaning that it is heritage that is recognized: the group who does it must acknowledge it as part of their culture.[6] Considering intangible cultural heritage shows that the world exists outside of what has been written down and documented: while much can be gained by knowing about the world through the documentary record, intangible cultural history shows the ways in which culture, while something that is adaptive and flexible, can also be something that can be endangered. Much intangible cultural heritage is something that is endangered by accident or through no malicious intent: the process stops being passed down, practitioners die and do not pass the trade on, the next generation has a desire to do something outside of the family trade, or certain trades become obsolete through modernization. Some intangible cultural heritage, it should be noted, is becoming more fragile and endangered because of systems of colonialism, capitalism, exploitative labor, or violence.

Some intangible cultural heritage is fragile and is on the verge of extinction. UNESCO argues that intangible cultural heritage is a vital resource that should be safeguarded, which includes "measures aimed at ensuring the viability of the intangible cultural heritage, including the identification, documentation, research, preservation, protection, promotion, enhancement, transmission, particularly through formal and nonformal education, as well as the revitalization of the various aspects of heritage."[7] When one focuses on safeguarding intangible culture, they work with the community who takes part in the intangible culture (or are part of the culture themselves) and work toward strategies for preservation of an important historic artifact. It's important to not think about the preservation of intangible cultural heritage through the lens of a sort of preciousness. Rather, it is an attempt to preserve something that is an important part of culture; it is something that dynamically tells us about the world and its people. It is something that tells us what it inherently means to be human.

Those practices from the past are not always a given, and the past we make is not a given. Rather, it is a small flame that needs to be cultivated. Historic shoemaker Shaun Pekar noted that, in many ways, the idea of the learning of a craft is an artifact, but it is a very complicated artifact. In discussing his passionate re-creation of the techniques of eighteenth-century shoemakers, Shaun noted, "If shoemaking is the artifact, there is just too much to it."[8] The knowledge of process is both tangible and intangible, something that can be put on a shelf or into the leaves of a book. But it is also something much bigger. In the context of a museum, museum professionals are used to the idea of the artifact that is held in the collection—but we can expand that.

An example that can illuminate this further is sign painting and hand-lettered signage. Hand-painted signs are part of many museum collections and could range from a tavern sign from the eighteenth century, to an advertisement from the twentieth. The advertising world of the past was a much more hands-on world than our modern one. Signage would have been made and crafted by the hand of an artist, who often experienced an apprenticeship to learn the trade. Signs could be a part of a museum's collection, but often just become a sign that blends into the background of storage. I choose this example, in part, because my grandfather was a sign painter and a billboard artist. While he was working at a local amusement park well into my life making hand-lettered signs, I never had the interest while he was alive to learn the process of hand lettering. This is a regret. Sign painters are a dying trade. They exist, and can be hired, but the career at large has been replaced by digital printing and more digital graphic design. While the signs in a museum collection are part of the collection itself, the people who made them (and the people who could make them as part of a living trade) are quickly falling away. Without some moves to help preserve the trade, soon there will be no sign painters. When there are none, the signs in our collections will become somewhat less decipherable: we will have lost something. We will have also lost something from the broader cultural landscape. A drive throughout the American countryside once rendered a world covered with signage hand painted by an artist. Today, not so much.

Change, of course, happens, but that part of our cultural heritage is quickly disintegrating. Unless work is done to study it, to preserve the materials connected to it, and to learn from it, some trades will be gone and will be harder for historians in the future to study. Those future historians will be much removed from them, and will have to look through a much murkier window to get to the realities of historic trades. For many of us who have sites that work with the nineteenth and twentieth centuries, those trades are right there. We know about them. We know how they work, so the onus falls to us to help preserve them.

Some of this ethos can be found in the historical precedent of Henry Mercer, of southeastern Pennsylvania. In the late nineteenth century, Mercer became increasingly concerned that industrialization was removing past knowledge of American life, and so he sought to create an encyclopedic collection of tools that are representative of historic trades and crafts. These preindustrial tools form the basis of the collection of the Mercer Museum, a concrete castle constructed by Mercer in Doylestown, Pennsylvania, which includes his vast (and eclectic) collection.[9] Mercer had resources available for the creation of a near encyclopedic historic trades collection and the building of a structure to contain it. Many of our historic sites do not. However, many of our collections contain materials that are very similar to Mercer's collection. My first historic site, the Red Mill Museum Village, in Clinton, New Jersey, contains a collection of over forty thousand objects, many of them connected to nineteenth-century trades. These tools exist in our collections. They are put on display and are talked about to the general public. If a museum is to take the maker ethos into its heart, part of the museum's goal should be understanding what these tools are and the processes they were a part of. Part of that goal should be working to understand and re-create some of those processes (with non-accessioned or replica tools, of course), to gain a deeper understanding of those processes and to help preserve the tangible reality of those processes for future generations.

I am advocating for tangibility and to use that tangibility as a tool of access to the past for people of the present. In thinking about making in a historical context, we also have to think about the intangible: the artifact part of historical process knowledge. We need to ask ourselves what it means to re-create a historic trade from the past, to become an expert in a historic trade, and to pass that trade on to others. In some ways, learning a dead trade makes one an interesting person to talk to at parties and a good partner to have on a trivia team: it brings with it a wide variety of random knowledge. It can be something that is a challenge, that pushes a maker in new and compelling ways. It can be something that helps one have a deeper understanding of the past and the people who lived in it. However, at its basest level, learning about a trade and attempting to re-create it is an attempt to preserve that fragile, intangible, cultural heritage. Not everyone might need to know how to make a barrel like an early nineteenth-century cooper, but doesn't humanity lose something if no one knows how a barrel could be made and was made in the past? Not everyone might be able to learn how to make a perfectly arranged hand-painted sign, but isn't humanity a touch poorer if that knowledge is gone forever, replaced only with materials printed from a large format printer?

Historic processes are vital elements of intangible cultural heritage that should be preserved. This work can be done in many places, but, as we will explore, one of the best places this can happen is in a museum, where historic process can be considered one more artifact that is held in the public trust, in addition to the more tangible artifacts in a museum's collection. If we are to see historic processes as an artifact that is part of a museum collection, we must expand the idea what a collection is and what it means. In a traditional sense, museum collections are objects and buildings. They are tangible pieces that museums and historic sites hold in the public trust, ensuring that they will be around for people both now and in the future. Museums care for, research, and interpret their collections for the public. This definition has a long history, reaching back to cabinets of curiosity and displays of objects of wealth and power. In these cases, the tangible object was the important thing: people needed to see objects, almost like relics, on the shelves that they encountered. This is a narrow definition of the culture of the past. It also disregards the humanity of the people who made the objects in museum collections. In the traditional sense of the cabinet of curiosities and old museum collections, those people were often "non-Western" people. In a more modern sense of the history museum, it could mean an unnamed craftsman. The object becomes a relic of the past, but it is disconnected from the dynamic lives that led to its creation. In considering the objects in museum collections as important cultural artifacts being held in the public trust, perhaps it should be equally important to consider the processes that made them as artifacts to be preserved as well. It would be impossible to accession a process, but the intangible cultural heritage of the processes that made the items in the collection is just as important as the tangible cultural heritage kept in museum collections throughout the country. Articulating processes as part of the culture being preserved in a museum does not require a massive shift in what a museum is or what a museum collection is, but it does create a meaningful change that allows for the preservation of the intangible history in our communities. It shifts thinking about collections as precious relics to thinking about them as something that was made by someone's hands. The sort of history that could, at a moment's notice, fade away. It also is a decentralizing act. Thinking about process allows us to think about and experience, in some way at least, the dynamic lives of the people who made the artifact. People who might have had different experiences from us, but people who were humans just like us.

WHERE ELSE BUT THE MUSEUM? WHO ELSE BUT MUSEUM PROFESSIONALS?

"Where else can you do these kinds of things but in a museum? Where else can you learn a historic trade?"[10] Shoemaker Shaun Pekar raised this rhetorical question to me in one of our conversations. Making is an important part of the history museum, but, likewise, the history museum is an important part of making. As has been explored throughout this book, making is not a new part of the museum experience; it has been there since the boom of museums throughout the United States around the bicentennial. These processes are part of visitor experiences (every time I do candle dipping at a museum event, there is always a parent or a grandparent who talks fondly of when they learned how to do it at a museum in their childhood). These moments at an event can act as an important bridge for getting generations to interact with each other.

We have already been doing it, but many of us do not necessarily think about what we're doing. Historic sites will employ historic trades at programming, but not necessarily consider what they are doing as part of the process of the preservation of a historic trade. Leave that, they would say (and have said to me), to Colonial Williamsburg; they're the people who know what they are doing. Colonial Williamsburg certainly does know what they are doing, but that does not mean they (and larger sites like them) need to hold the monopoly on the preservation of historic trades. Many museums (especially small ones) do not have the resources for storing their collections according to best practices and best procedures like somewhere such as the Smithsonian or the Metropolitan Museum of Art might be able to. But, as texts on collection storage will note, good is better than not at all. If historic processes are intangible cultural heritage, it is our duty to preserve them in the same ways that we preserve our collection. With limited availability of resources that might just have to be good enough. But it's better than nothing.

This is particularly important because the stakes are high. Sign painting, the historic dying trade I have some kinship to, is not the only trade to be on its deathbed. There is little in place to save them. In the United States (where this book was written), there is no formal governmental program for the preservation of trades or of intangible cultural heritage. In other countries, such as the United Kingdom, projects such as the Heritage Craft Association provide funding for the learning and maintenance of historic crafts, and update yearly their Red List of Endangered Crafts, which notes crafts that are at risk of disappearance. At-risk crafts are identified as either critically endangered ("those at serious risk of no longer being practiced in the UK") or endangered ("currently have sufficient craftspeople to transmit the craft skills to the next generation, but for which there are serious concerns about their ongoing viability").[11] The Heritage Craft Association, then, provides grant funding and resources for the maintenance of crafts throughout the commonwealth, ensuring the historic preservation of the craft for the future.

The United States, too, does have some of these structures in place. Programs such as the Traditional Trades Advancement Program (TTAP) run through the National Park Service in Fredericksburg, Maryland, work to keep traditional skills such as carpentry, woodcrafting, masonry, and metalworking alive for use in restorations and construction.[12] Likewise, granting programs are available through the National Endowment for the Arts for projects related to folk and traditional arts, including music, dance, craft, and oral expression.[13] Museums such as Mystic Seaport work to keep the traditional skills and trades of the shipyard alive and dynamic in the modern world. These programs are important and go a long way toward the preservation of this valuable intangible cultural heritage. But, alone, they are not sufficient. There is a great need for larger structures advocating preservation and for more funding toward preservation.

If we are to be passionate about the making that is occurring in our history museums, we should also be passionate about the crafts that are being learned in our makerspaces—those intangible cultural heritage processes that connect our makers to the past—and museums should also realize that, at least in the United States, they represent one of the main lines of defense against the death of heritage trades and crafts. Museums and historic sites can make several steps toward the cultivation and preservation of historic trades and crafts. Here are some ideas:

- Have a well-considered and sustainability funded makerspace, where people can experiment with historic trades and crafts.
- Work on cultivating a cohort of makers, who work together at your museum and in your makerspace. The idea of learning together as a community is incredibly important. Kristie Truluck, executive director of Maine's First Ship, an organization that created a reconstruction of the *Virginia*, noted that the whole project was an example of "a group of people who got together and said what happens if we build a ship? How will we do it? How will we pay for it? Let's figure it out!"[14] For Maine's First Ship, this cohort of questioners led to the creation of an entire site which functioned as a makerspace for the creation of a seventeenth-century sailing vessel. The resource of people is incredibly important, as is the cultivation of people.

- Funding is also exceptionally important. If attempting to aid in the preservation of historic trades and crafts is important for your site, put your money where your mouth is. Of course, money is always a precious resource at any historic site. However, well-placed funding can go a long way. This can be the funding of makerspace projects, but it could also be things such as creating a grant program for historic makers or people that want to be a historic maker. Likewise, your organization could take a page out of arts organizations' books and fund a maker-in-residency program, where your organization could temporarily fund someone to come and learn or hone a historic trade or craft in your makerspace. This could be developed into apprenticeship programs, which can be found in places like Colonial Williamsburg, Mystic Seaport, and the Eli Whitney Museum and Workshop.
- Work toward having an organizational knowledge and understanding of what it means to preserve intangible cultural heritage.
- Make times for makers to talk: just as we have talked about how makerspaces do not exist in a vacuum, so, too, the preservation of trades does not occur in a vacuum. Find others who are doing the same thing and talk about the process, hold events for makers within your region, share information.
- Create a space where diverse makers from the community can come together to preserve cultural heritage. Heritage can be potentially problematic: Whose heritage? Who belongs and who doesn't? Ensure that your organization does not have a one-sided, or too narrow, version of what heritage is. Heritage can be easily weaponized and can be easily brought into languages of white supremacy and the supporting of exploitive systems of power and control. Avoid this, but also acknowledge this. Bringing in diverse makers from your community can make you aware of trades or crafts that are being made by minorities in your community. Bring in many voices and cast a wide net of makers and people passionate about making.

Some of what makes the museum such an important place for the learning of historic trades and crafts comes from the unique position of the museum. Truly, there is really no place where one could be paid to learn a historic trade or craft as part of one's normal job, and then have the unique privilege of showing that skill to visitors to help them gain a deeper knowledge of the past.

The museum in general is already perfectly situated to be deployed as an essential tool for the preservation of intangible cultural heritage. Likewise, it is perfectly situated to be a place where that intangible cultural heritage can be used to ask new questions of the past. The makerspace at your historic site can do just that. It is far more than a programming gimmick, and far more than just a way to get people through the door. Making is an ethos, as is the makerspace. Historical making is an ethos as well.

One of the founding threads of this book is that making is something that brands us as inherently human. To make something with our hands, to feel a raw material move between our fingers, to will something into being from "be-inglessness" puts us in touch with our humanity. While making can ennoble us, elevate us, or inspire us, it shows us the tangible, physical reality of the human experience. To learn a craft from the past connects us with the humans who have come before. It contextualizes us and grounds us, and, more importantly, shows the past as something that was lived, by real people just like us. Real people who, like us, made things with their hands. Real people who were, after all, humans just like we are.

DO!

The historic makerspace can help make museums and historic sites an accessible, enjoyable, and historically rich place for the communities in which they reside. They can help sites engage with new visitors and new constituencies. Most importantly, they can help question and challenge existing narratives of power and colonialism found in the museum itself.

In ending, it is important to remind you of the main ethos that this book has been arguing toward. Our historic makerspaces should be a place to encourage making and encourage the visitors and makers who work there to try, experiment, get their hands dirty. To make. They should also, though, be a place where failure is embraced and learned from, where the process of learning is acknowledged not as something that happens in a short time but that happens through experimentation, practice, and failure.

With that in mind: make a historic makerspace. Make a large historic makerspace that changes the way that people interact with your site. Make a small historic makerspace that is a cart that rolls out sometimes or a smaller historic makerspace that comes out for one program a year. Try a workshop. Try to learn a skill. Try to teach a skill. Try. Do. Make. Twentieth-century artist Sol LeWitt wrote to the artist Eva Hesse in 1965, one artist trying to encourage another out of a block. LeWitt wrote, "Just stop thinking, worrying, looking over your shoulder, wondering, doubting, fearing, hurting, hoping for some easy way out, struggling, grasping, confusing, itching, scratching, mumbling, bumbling, grumbling, humbling . . . besmirching, grinding, grinding, grinding, grinding away at yourself. Stop it and just do!"[15] A historic makerspace is an important investment and change in the way your site will interact with the public. It will require much thought, much consultation with your site and the community, much consideration about how it will fit into the broader structure of your site itself. But, in the end, like LeWitt said, you just must do.

This book was about giving you the tools. Now, go out there and make something.

NOTES

1. Roeland Paardekooper and Jodi Reeves Flores, "Histories of Experimental Archeology: Documenting the Past for the Future," in Jodi Reeves Flores and Roeland Paardekooper, eds., *Experiments Past: Histories of Experimental Archaeology*, 7 (Leiden: Sidestone Press, 2014).
2. Frederick W. F. Foulds, "Introduction," in Frederick W. F. Foulds, ed., *Experimental Archaeology and Theory: Recent Approaches to Archaeological Hypotheses*, 1 (Oxford and Oakville: Oxbow Books, 2013).
3. "KSUEAL (Kent State University Experimental Archaeology Laboratory)," Kent State University, https://sites.google.com/view/ksuexarchlab/home?authuser=0.
4. Frederick W. F. Foulds, "Introduction," in Frederick W. F. Foulds, ed., *Experimental Archaeology and Theory*, 1.
5. "Text of the Convention for the Safeguarding of the Intangible Cultural Heritage," UNESCO. Accessed February 3, 2022. https://ich.unesco.org/en/convention #art2.
6. Ibid.
7. Ibid.
8. Shaun Pekar, historic shoemaker, in discussion with the author, January 13, 2022.
9. "About: The Mercer Museum," The Mercer Museum, https://www.mercermuseum .org/collections/mercer-museum/.
10. Ibid.
11. "Craft Skills under Threat with 27 Additions to the HCA Red List of Endangered Crafts." Heritage Crafts, October 10, 2021. https://heritagecrafts.org.uk/craft-skills -under-threat-with-27-additions-to-the-hca-red-list-of-endangered-crafts/.
12. "What is TTAP?" The Campaign for Historic Trades. https://historictrades.org.
13. "Grants for Arts Projects: Folk and Traditional Arts," National Endowment for the Arts. https://www.arts.gov/grants/grants-for-arts-projects/folk-traditional-arts.
14. Kristie Truluck, executive director, Maine's First Ship, in discussion with the author, January 19, 2022.
15. Katherine Brooks, "An Artist's Harsh Advice Is What Every Creative Person Needs to Hear," HuffPost, October 28, 2015. https://www.huffpost.com/entry/eva -hesse-letters-sol-lewitt_n_562f79ede4b00aa54a4b18d8.

Appendices

The following resources have been put together to help guide you along your makerspace journey. Feel free to take them and adapt them to the needs of your makerspace and your organization. As with everything in this book, they are a guide to get you started and to get you making!

APPENDIX A

Making and Your Site: Assessment Worksheet

What kind of making do we do at our site already?

When does making happen at our site?

Is there anything that connects to the history of our site that ties to making? (Was making done here in the past? Were the people connected to this place makers? Do we have a particularly robust material culture collection? etc.)

What kind of making would we like to do?

In what contexts should making happen at our site?

APPENDIX B

Your Mission and Your Makerspace

What is your organization's mission?

What, in the history of your site, is connected to making?

How does making relate to your organization's mission? Does it?

How would making improve your ability to reach your community via your mission?

What would a maker program do to improve your site?

What are some possible risks?

APPENDIX C

Historic Makerspace Sample Budget

Here is a sample budget form you can use to figure out the cost of a potential makerspace. Table C.1 is for considering opening a historic makerspace, but it can be easily adapted into a departmental budget. Add whatever categories are necessary. Talk to whoever does your organization's finances to see their preferred formatting for budgets.

Income	Budgeted	YTD
Organizational Support		
Sponsorship		
Tickets/Admission		
Total Income		
Expenses		
Materials		
Equipment		
Furniture		
Lighting		
Storage		
Advertising		
Misc.		
Total Expenses		

APPENDIX D

Makerspace User Agreement

Having a makerspace user agreement can be a good option for your site. The extent of the user agreement can depend on the needs of your site. Some user agreements include information such as a hold harmless agreement; others do not.

Here is an example of a basic user agreement:

OLD HOUSE HISTORIC MAKERSPACE USER AGREEMENT

As a user of the Old House Historic Makerspace, I will respect others, respect the historic makerspace, and be a safe member of the maker community. I agree that I will:

- Respect everyone and their ideas, and:
  a. Be respectful of differences, other ideas, or other ways of doing things.
  b. Work to ensure that the historic makerspace is a friendly environment free of bullying, harassment, and intimidation.
- Respect the historic makerspace, and:
  a. Leave your space cleaner than when you found it.
  b. Ensure that tools, equipment, and unused materials are returned to where they came from.
  c. Dispose of trash, recycling, and other refuse in designated containers.
- Be a safe member of the maker community. I will:
  a. Wear the appropriate protective gear and follow the historic makerspace dress code. Avoiding clothing that does not hang from the body or is loose in any way, dangling jewelry (necklaces, bracelets, etc.) should be avoided.
  b. Use appropriate personal protective equipment (PPE).
  c. Refrain from alcohol and drug use while using the makerspace.

In signing this document, I acknowledge that I will adhere to the user agreement above and recognize that violating any of the above will result in my not being able to use the Old House Historic Makerspace.

Signed: _____

Print: _____

Date: _____

Phone Number: _____

Email: _____

APPENDIX E

INVENTORY

Completing a regular inventory of your historic makerspace can ensure that funds are well spent and resources are well allocated. Table E.1 shows a sample inventory sheet that can be easily replicated in the spreadsheet program of your choice to take an inventory of your tools, material, and more.

Item	Storage Bin/Shelf #	Number on Hand	Notes/Condition/Misc.

APPENDIX F

RECIPES AND PROJECTS

Starting a historic makerspace and not knowing what to make in it can be daunting and frustrating. Here are some recipes and projects to get your makerspace started. They are adaptable, accessible, and fun. Try them, add them to your maker repertoire, and then add some more!

WALNUT INK

Walnuts have long been used to make ink, especially in places where walnut trees grow. If your site has a bunch of black walnut trees, what better way to deal with the problem of black walnuts than to make ink out of them?

Tools and Materials You Will Need:
- Black walnuts (a dozen is a good number; walnuts that have begun to blacken are ideal. I have also had success with walnuts that I have let rot in a pot outside—this allows for the nuts to oxidize and darken)
- A pot (this should be a pot that you wouldn't use for food or anything else, as it will stain)
- A wooden spoon (again, this will stain with the walnuts)
- A preservative (vinegar or gum arabic work very well)
- A heat source (this works great over a kitchen fire or an outdoor fire, but it also works just as well with a portable heater or a kitchen stovetop)
- A metal sieve strainer

Process:
1. Place black walnuts into a pot, and cover them with water.
2. Bring water in the pot to a simmer, and leave it simmering for 8 hours. The liquid should become dark black and thicker.
3. Strain the boiled water through a sieve to remove larger particles and materials. I like to strain this into a mason jar. A similar container with a lid will work just fine.
4. Add a preservative: this is especially important if you are going to bottle the ink or use it another time. This can be either a teaspoon of vinegar or a teaspoon of gum arabic. Close the container and gently shake it, to incorporate the ink throughout.

Walnut ink can be used for a variety of applications; it can even be used as a quick and simple die or as a wood stain. The most common application can be through teaching quill and ink writing.

VICTORIAN MOURNING JEWELRY

This is the process that I described in chapter 5 of this book. It is based on my own personal research, using a plethora of sources.

Tools and Materials You Will Need:
- A foot-long lock of hair (I used doll hair, but any hair is perfectly fine)
- Gum arabic
- Wire (copper wire is ideal and seems to be the one used most historically, though you can use a wire that matches the color of the hair you are using. Cut to a length of 2 feet)
- A dowel (I've found the easiest way is with a dowel cut to around a foot long. Any thickness will work: thinner means more difficult and a tighter curl)
- Tape (this is a modern addition which makes the project a bit easier, especially for the beginner)

Process:
1. Select a strand of hair. The ideal width is somewhere between 15 and 25 strands of hair.
2. Using the gum arabic, attach the ends of the hair together, so that they are held together in a bundle. Coat the strands around a quarter of an inch.
3. Fold your wire in half. Crease it at the fold. Hold the fold in the wire and where you joined pieces of hair next to each other.
4. Wrap the wire and the hair around the dowel, securing it to one end of the dowel. You can tape this in place, to ensure that it doesn't move around.
5. Hold the dowel with your nondominant hand. The hair can fall freely, but a wire should be on both sides of the dowel, pointing away from you.
6. Wrap the hair around the dowel once. Take the left wire and cross it in front of the hair, then cross the right wire over the left wire and the hair. The wire should hold the hair into place.
7. Repeat step 6 until you almost run out of hair. It is important that you repeat the process (wrap in the same direction, and cross one wire first and then the other). Deviation from that pattern will work, but it will result in a less neat piece of hair work.
8. When you are nearing the end of the strand, but still have some left over, wrap around the dowel and cross the wires as you had been previously. Then take the remaining wire and tightly wrap it around the remaining hair, to secure it.
9. If you have taped the hair and wire to the dowel, remove the tape. Carefully slide the wrapped hair off the dowel. It should maintain its shape (it will be like a long, tight curl).
10. You can take the curl of hair you made and form it into shapes, using the wire. Traditionally, this could be used for the petals of flowers.

PAINT

Modern people often view paint as something that comes out of a tube. Historically, that was not the case. Before the invention of paint made in factories for mass production, paint would have been made by the batch and then used by an artist.

Any paint follows a basic rule of thumb: paint is made up of pigment and binder. In this case, pigment is dry pigment. Dry pigments can be ordered from a craft supply store or dry pigments can be foraged, which is a process where one collects pigments from the ground or the environment and uses them to make paint. For the beginner (or someone who wants to have more control over the colors in their collection), store-bought pigments are ideal. For more advanced painters, pigment foraging could be a way to go.

EGG TEMPERA PAINT

Egg tempera is an ancient way of painting, and involves using egg yolk and pigment and then painting with the resultant mixture.

Tools and Materials You Will Need:
- Eggs (this is dependent on how much you would like to paint: one egg goes further than you will expect it to)
- Water
- Dry pigments
- Material to paint on (thick watercolor paper is good for an egg tempera painting program, but gessoed [prepared] wood is ideal)
- Paintbrushes
- A small cup
- A palette for mixing
- A palette knife

Process:
1. Carefully break the egg and separate the white from the yolk. Be careful to not break the yolk (room temperature eggs work best).
2. Over a small cup, break the yolk sack and separate out the membrane.
3. Add water to the small cup to dilute the egg yolk: a ratio of 1:1 works well. This is the binder for your pigment.
4. Add a small amount of each dry pigment to either a palette or to individual cups. Add the egg yolk and water mixture to the pigment, enough that it becomes paintable, but not too "liquidy." Mix using a palette knife, until smooth. Optionally, you may use a muller or grinder to grind pigments.
5. Paint as normal. Egg tempera dries very quickly.
6. Clean up with soap and water.

OIL PAINT

Oil paint originated during the Northern Renaissance and proved to be the standard with which artists would make art: it would be a favorite for American miniature painters and portraitists. Oil paint uses oil, usually linseed oil, instead of egg as the binder.

Tools and Materials You Will Need:
- Linseed oil
- Dry pigments
- Material to paint on (prepared canvas is ideal)
- Paintbrushes
- A small cup
- A palette for mixing
- A palette knife
- Paint thinner or turpentine

Process:
1. Add a small amount of each dry pigment to either a palette or to individual cups.
2. Add linseed oil to the pigment, enough that it becomes paintable, but not too "liquidy." Mix using a palette knife, until smooth. Optionally, you may use a muller or grinder to grind pigments.
3. Paint. Oil paint has a very slow drying time. To dilute paint, use either linseed oil or paint thinner.
4. Clean up with paint thinner, followed by soap and water.

APPENDIX G

PROGRAMS

Once you have a historic makerspace, what do you do at it? Here are walk-through guides for two basic historic makerspace programs: the drop-in workshop and the history happy hour. They are adaptable and scalable to your site and its needs; try them out, and use them as a jumping-off point for trying more!

DROP-IN WORKSHOP (FAMILIES)

The drop-in workshop is a great way to provide a space for making for the community and to get them involved in your makerspace. It also introduces the idea of making a stress-free environment.

A drop-in workshop is scheduled for a certain period of time and people can stop by within that time frame to take part in the workshop. The goal is for it to be a short interaction rather than a long day. Ideally, they work into a family's busy schedule on the weekend, providing a stop and something to do. While they work very well for families, anyone can enjoy a drop-in workshop.

MATERIALS, SUPPLIES, AND LOCATION

The materials and supplies for a drop-in workshop are dependent on whatever craft you want to teach at it. Here are some things you should consider:

- The goal of a drop-in workshop is that people can just drop in and learn about and make something. When considering crafts that you can do at the workshop, they should be shorter and require minimal explanation. Likewise, they should be exciting and accessible for a wide variety of makers (or, at least, scalable, depending on the audience at your table at the moment).
- While much of this book emphasizes the value and importance of providing a space for failure, in choosing a drop-in workshop craft, think about crafts that have a high success rate. For many people taking part in your drop-in workshop, this will be the first time they are accessing making at your site. Make it a positive experience to encourage their maker appetite.

Other materials include, as needed:

- a table and a tablecloth (if you are having this outside or in a space that is not your makerspace)
- a garbage can
- a tent (if you are having it outside)

The point of a drop-in workshop is for people to be able to drop in and try something on their schedule. These work really well as an outside project, near where people can park. Likewise, they could be something that is in a gallery space or in a building on your site. They can also be taken on the road (I've done drop-in workshops at large public gatherings). You could also have them in your historic makerspace. In short: they fit anywhere.

EXPENSES

As with materials, the expenses here depend on the process that you are using.

A drop-in workshop could be anything, but the thing about them is that it is difficult to tell if you will have a lot of people or no people at all. As a result, drop-in workshops are very successful when the materials that are being used are cheaper rather than expensive. Likewise, if you are planning a series of drop-in workshops, it is beneficial to think about crafts that work well together or that use the same materials, so you can buy materials in bulk (therefore cheaper).

Other expenses depend on the budget of your site. Some advertising never hurts (for drop-in workshops, online advertising in local online calendars or on social media can be particularly helpful). It can also be worth purchasing lawn signs or a banner to advertise the workshop. When it comes to advertising, work to fit your budget for drop-in workshop advertising into the broader advertising strategies of your organization.

ADMISSION

People can pay for your drop-in workshop in a variety of ways; this can depend on your organization and the goals of your organization. Here are some possibilities:

- As part of site admission. The drop-in workshop could be included with admission to your site. This is great if it is something that occurs within the site (if people who are taking part in it must enter your site), likewise it can be used as a way to increase visitation to the site. A downside, potentially, could be that this could limit the number of families who might take part in it (some might not want to pay full museum admission for the entire family for something that they are planning to just drop in for).
- As a separate admission. A drop-in workshop could be a separate admission than the site admission, which could mean that people could opt to do it or not. Likewise, they could opt to do it and not visit the rest of the site. Logistically, this can be a challenge and limits where the drop-in workshop could take place (it would have to be somewhere near an entrance to the site rather than elsewhere).

- As a donation ("pay as you want"). A drop-in workshop could be a separate donation, operating as a "pay as you want" system. This can be great, but is unpredictable. Sometimes people are more generous this way and might donate more money than is expected. As with a separate admission, this limits where the drop-in could be located, if you want it to be something that is accessed by people who might not necessarily be taking part in the actual museum tour.
- As a membership perk. The drop-in workshop could be something that is a perk of being a museum member, and people could take part in it by showing proof of membership. This could be good in that it could increase membership, but could be bad in that it makes the drop-in something that
  - is more exclusive or not available for people who might not necessarily be able to afford membership prices. This option could be paired with others: the drop-in workshop could have a minor expense but be free to museum members as a perk of membership.
- Free. The drop-in workshop could also be free. This might be a necessity for sites that do not charge admission (such as government sites). Likewise, it could work for a site that has a healthier budget or a sponsor who is willing to underwrite the cost of the drop-in workshop program.

In thinking about admission for drop-in workshops, I encourage you to think about the broader ways in which you want the drop-in workshop to work. Is it something to engage your community, to make them excited, and to interact with new constituents? In that case, free or by donation might be better. Is it something that you want to think about as a program in addition to other programs? Then a payment system might be a good idea. Think of your site's needs, your community's needs, and what you would like to get out of the program as a whole.

INCENTIVIZE REPEAT VISITS

If you are planning on having a series of drop-in workshops, consider creating a punch card system (like you'd get at a frozen yogurt stand) or something similar to track repeat visitors. Reward repeat visitors with a prize (a toy from the gift shop, a special sticker, etc.). It's a small token, but it can make the process seem valuable and fun, and also rewards those who are making an investment into coming to your site. Don't be afraid, too, to use the drop-in workshop as a way to increase interest in your makerspace and your site in general.

STAFF

Staffing the workshop is very dependent on what your site's resources are and what the program looks like. A drop-in workshop can be successful with just one person manning the table, but two people can be even more helpful. It is important, though, that at least one of those people has a very solid understanding of whatever craft you are teaching at the drop-in workshop.

PROGRAM AND HOW TO DO IT

Here is a step-by step guide to preparing for your drop-in workshop that you can follow.

Before the drop-in workshop:

- Plan and advertise the event. Select a date and a time. If you are planning on having a series of drop-in workshops, it works very well to select a day and time that is consistent (for example, you could do drop-in workshops on the first and third Saturdays of each month, from noon to 4 p.m.). With this sort of standardization, you can easily tell people when the next one will be.
- Plan the craft ahead of time and advertise the craft so that people know what to expect. Often, this works well if it is somewhat themed to the season or to something that could be seen inside the museum: tie-ins to exhibits are excellent, too!
- Make sure that you have the proper materials on hand before the day of the drop-in workshop. Organizing the materials and doing any pre-preparation of the materials before the day of the workshop can be very helpful.

Day of the drop-in workshop:

- Set up the table and prepare the space as well as possible before the beginning of the drop-in workshop. Make sure that everything is ready to go if someone decides to drop-in right at the beginning.
- It can be very helpful to do a demo craft, for people to see what it is they are making: making that at the beginning of the day of the workshop can also reacquaint you with the process and provide you time to teach anyone the process that is going to also be working at the table.

HISTORY HAPPY HOUR (ADULTS)

History happy hours take the idea of the drop-in workshop and expand it, turning it into an evening that adults will enjoy at your museum or historic site. At these events, visitors can learn a craft and enjoy your site in a happy hour–style event. History happy hours are nothing new for historic sites, but this version takes the idea and gives it a maker spin.

MATERIALS, SUPPLIES, AND LOCATION

The materials and supplies for a history happy hour depend on whatever craft you want to teach at it. Here are some things you should consider:

- The goal of the history happy hour is to provide a space for adults to learn something new. When considering crafts that you can do at these functions, they should be shorter and require minimal explanation. Likewise, they should be exciting and accessible for a wide variety of makers with a variety of different skill sets (or, at least, scalable, depending on the audience at your table at the moment).

- When you are considering crafts, be cognizant of tools and equipment that might have to be used. Successful and safe history happy hours steer away from using equipment that someone might hurt themselves with if they have had a drink or two. If you want to do something that requires more mental acuity, consider having beverages after the craft.
- While much of this book emphasizes the value and importance of providing a space for failure, in choosing a history happy hour craft, think about crafts that have a high success rate. For many people taking part in your history happy hour, this will be the first time they are accessing making at your site. Make it a positive experience to whet their maker appetite.

FOOD AND DRINK

The history happy hour is successful, in part, because it creates a space for adults to play. Think of it as a regular happy hour with a craft attached to it.

Drink

- Offer both alcoholic and non-alcoholic options for your guests. It is also a good idea to include water as an option as well.
- Themed cocktails can be a great touch: there are a lot of really interesting historic cocktail recipes out in the world.
- Drink can be a good opportunity to make a friendship and partnership for your organization in the community: Is there a local brewery or winery near your historic site? Maybe you already partner with them: Perhaps they would be interested in sponsoring the event?

Food

- Food at a history happy hour is not a meal, but it is a necessary addition to the alcoholic beverages you will be serving. Think of food as appetizers and samplers.
- It can be fun to theme food to your site or to the topic at hand. If you're doing a history happy hour about a process that was popular in the 1950s, why not try 1950s party recipes?
- This can also be a good opportunity to find a partnership with a local restaurant or food purveyor.

Other materials include, as needed:

- a table and a tablecloth (if you are having this outside or in a space that is not your makerspace)

- a garbage can
- a tent (if you are having it outside)

A history happy hour is a good excuse to show off your site as well as your maker program. On a good day, a history happy hour is great outside (if the equipment you are using for it can be taken there). It can also work very well in a gallery or in your historic makerspace. Remember to allow time for your guests to mingle and to explore your site.

EXPENSES

As with materials, the expenses here depend on the process that you are using, so just as with the drop-in workshops, consider your overall budget as well as your overall supply inventory.

Another series of expenses include the food and the drink that is a part of the event. Consider budgeting the cost of food and drink into the cost of the ticket price for the event.

Other expenses depend on the budget of your site. Some advertising never hurts (for history happy hour events, online advertising in local online calendars or on social media can be particularly helpful). It can also be worth purchasing lawn signs or a banner to advertise the happy hour. When it comes to advertising, work to fit your budget for the history happy hour advertising into the broader advertising strategies of your organization.

ADMISSION

History happy hours work best as a pre-ticketed event. Consider the craft, your site's capabilities, the space available, and your staff and set a number of tickets for the event. Factor in the cost of supplies and food, as well as the cost of other events that your site does, and then set a ticket price. Make purchasing tickets as easy as possible: an online option, while there will be a surcharge, is always a good idea.

If you are planning on having a series of history happy hours, consider a reduced rate if someone buys tickets for the whole series.

STAFF

Staffing for a history happy hour is dependent on the site's resources and your staff. It's also somewhat dependent on your site itself. At the least, having two people works well, but be sure you have people to cover the following (it can be the same people):

- Check in, checking tickets, etc.
- Running the workshop and teaching the craft
- Helping people learn the craft
- Manning the food and drink tables

- Answering questions about your site and managing traffic flow within your site
- Ensuring the security of your historic museum and collections

PROGRAM AND HOW TO DO IT

Here is a step-by-step guide to preparing for your history happy hour that you can follow.

Before the drop-in workshop:

- Plan and advertise the event. Select a date and a time. If you are planning on having a series of history happy hours, it works very well to select a day and time that is consistent (such as the third Friday of the month in the evening). With this sort of standardization, you can easily tell people when the next one will be.
- Plan the craft ahead of time and advertise the craft so that people know what to expect. Often, this works well if it is somewhat themed to the season or to something that could be seen inside the museum: tie-ins to exhibits are excellent, too! Advertise, too, that the event is for adults of drinking age.
- Make sure that you have the proper materials on hand before the day of the history happy hour. Organizing the materials and doing any pre-preparation of the materials before the day of the happy hour can be very helpful.
- Plan the food and drink and make sure they will be ready and available for the day of the event. It is also a good idea to list ingredients. Be sure that you have the necessary serving things you will need (cups, plates, napkins, etc.).
- Set up a flow for the event: What happens and when? Where?

Day of the history happy hour:

- Pick up food and drink; prepare them and make sure they are ready for go-time.
- Purchase ice, if necessary.
- Prepare the space, set up any necessary tables, chairs, and equipment.
- Make available for staff a will-call list of who has purchased tickets and have it available at the check-in location.
- Before visitors arrive, set up food and drink.
- Before visitors arrive, have a meeting with whoever is working the event with you (volunteers or staff) and go over any questions.
- It can be very helpful to do a demo craft, for people to see what it is they are making: making that at the beginning of the day can also reacquaint you

with the process and provide you time to teach anyone the process that is going to also be working at the event.

At the event:

- Check people in and be sure they arrive to where they need to be. Explain to them the order of the evening. ("We're going to learn how to make a Victorian hair wreath. Before and after that, please help yourself to some refreshments. Afterward, you can explore our site.")
- Do the event as planned. It can be helpful to allow guests to mingle a bit and enjoy some refreshments, then do the making, then give them time to have more refreshments and explore: this breaks it up, makes it a social event, and allows them a space to get to know each other and the site.

Index

About the Author

Tim Betz is a museum professional, historian, and artist. He is executive director of the Morgan Log House, a historical society in Lansdale, Pennsylvania. He is an instructor of art history at Kutztown University of Pennsylvania and is completing his PhD in history at Lehigh University, in Bethlehem, Pennsylvania.

He is particularly interested in historic processes and historic craft, which he uses as a tool for understanding the past.